THE LONG

By the same author:

Uit die binneland (2005)
Anderkant die scrap (2006)
Op die agterpaaie (2008)
On the Back Roads (2008)
Op die toneel (2009)
Hiervandaan – Op reis in die geliefde land (2011)

Dana Snyman

The Long Way Home

A Journey Through South Africa

Tafelberg

For Ingrid

Tafelberg
an imprint of NB Publishers, 40 Heerengracht, Cape Town
www.tafelberg.com
© 2012 (Dana Snyman)

Translator: Erla Rabe
Editors: Roxanne Reid and Lynda Gilfillan
Proofreader: Linette Viljoen
Book design: Nazli Jacobs
Cover design: Anton Sassenberg
Cover photograph: Dana Snyman
Author photograph on back cover: Nardus Nel
Map by Izak Vollgraaff
Set in Egyptienne F by Nielfa Cassiem-Carelse
Printed and bound by Paarl Media, Paarl
First edition 2012
ISBN: 978-0-624-05487-0
e-Pub: 978-0-624-05800-7

How much past can the present bear?
— Ivan Vladislavić

Dana's journey

Contents

PART I

Roots

It looks like rain. I turn in at the farm gate just before Franschhoek. The road to the farmstead has been tarred and runs through vineyards, past a little church and a small cemetery.

I drive slower and slower under the low-hanging clouds.

Up to now, this farm has been no more to me than a name in books and documents in the archives in Cape Town, but now that I'm here I feel a bit like the prodigal son returning home after many years.

On my left, an earth dam; on my right, stables.

This is an authentic, traditional Boland farmyard. I notice that immediately. The house has a bunch of grapes on the gable, a thatched roof and wooden shutters in front of the windows. The wine cellar is to the side, surrounded by oak trees. Near a small building that looks like a security guard's office, a large blue-and-white signpost has been planted in the ground:

WELCOME TO SOLMS DELTA

Parking

Wine tasting

Museum

Restaurant

There's a tour bus and a few cars in the parking area opposite the restaurant. I pull in next to the bus but don't get out right away. The blue-and-white signpost draws my attention again. It looks out of place.

Once upon a time, more than three hundred years ago, this farm belonged to Christoffel Snyman, the original ancestor of all Snymans. Christoffel and his wife Margot lived here all their married life. Their nine children were born here and it was here that Christoffel died in 1709.

You could say this is where all of us Snymans come from: Oupa and Pa and me, and all those who came before us and all those who will come after us.

I feel like phoning Pa from my cellphone, but for the past two days it's been difficult to have a coherent telephone conversation with him. He's tired all the time and struggles to breathe. His heart is worn out. Yesterday evening, when I mentioned that I'd been to the archives and discovered that we're all descendants of Christoffel Snyman, and that I was going to visit the farm today, he responded by telling me about his great-great-grandpa who lived in Pietermaritzburg – the man who took part in the Great Trek and fought in the Battle of Blood River, the one whose names he bears: Coenraad Frederik Wilhelmus Snyman. This oupa Coenraad is the only long-ago Snyman I've ever heard him mention.

I get out of the bakkie. I always feel awkward when I visit a farm like this where I can walk around and eat and drink and do whatever I like, without knowing the owners or anyone on it.

Next to the restaurant there's a tall, narrow building with a wooden staircase on one side that leads to the loft. It looks as though it may once have been a cellar. A man emerges and comes over, a well-rehearsed greeting on his lips: "Good morning, sir. Welcome. Would you like to taste some of our excellent wine?"

He's one of the guides on the farm. Leon Adams. When I mention I'm a Snyman, he smiles. "Everything's inside. Come, let me show you." He pushes open the door to the building.

It opens into a large room where a dark table stands in the middle of the floor. Wine is sold in a smaller room to the side. There are wall panels depicting the history of the farm in words, sketches and old photographs. The first panel contains a single paragraph:

Museum Van de Caab tells the story of Delta farm. Similar stories could be told of all the old farms in this valley. The things that happened here reflect the whole history of South Africa.

Leon puts his hands together, palm to palm, almost like a minister in a pulpit, and begins to tell me of the San and Khoi, the first people to have lived here in the Groot Drakenstein Valley between Franschhoek and Paarl. Then he comes to 1657 . . . "You see, sir, in 1657 a woman by the name of Groot Catrijn was sent from Batavia to the Cape." He looks at me closely. "This Groot Catrijn was a convict, you know – a woman convict. She'd killed her boyfriend over there, so they sent her to Robben Island. For life."

Is he sure? Was she really banished to Robben Island? I ask. This contradicts what I read in the archives: Groot Catrijn van der Caab, a woman of Indian descent, was indeed banished to the Cape in 1657 after murdering her lover, but she went to work at the Castle as one of Jan van Riebeeck's washerwomen.

Leon wavers. He calls one of the guides from the sales room. "Tiaan!"

A man with a thin moustache comes over. Tiaan Jacobs.

"Did they send Groot Catrijn to Robben Island?" Leon asks.

"No, man. She became Jan van Riebeeck's washerwoman." Tiaan comes over and picks up the story. "You see, sir, it was there at the Castle that she met Hans Christoffel Schneider. He was like Van Riebeeck's personal bodyguard. The two of them, this Hans Christoffel Schneider and Groot Catrijn . . . they . . . they sort of had a relationship and nine months later she gave birth to Schneider's child."

That's more or less what I read in the archives in Cape Town: Groot Catrijn, the exile from Batavia, had a child out of wedlock and the father was Hans Christoffel Schneider, a German soldier at the Castle. Groot Catrijn called the boy Christoffel, and because the Cape was under Dutch rule, "Schneider" became "Snyman" in the public records. Christoffel Snyman.

"That's why people say he was the first Snyman, this Christoffel.

The very, very first Snyman." Tiaan points to another panel. "That's his signature."

I approach. There it is, behind glass: a copy of Christoffel Snyman's signature as it appeared on the deed of sale way back when. It's the handwriting of someone who could write properly, complete with curlicues.

Tiaan and his thin moustache are still by my side. "You know about this Christoffel, sir?" he says. "You know he wasn't white, don't you, sir?"

I see the shadowy reflection of my face in the glass. It's true. There's no denying it. Christoffel Snyman wasn't white; Groot Catrijn was a dark-skinned woman of Indian descent.

Our forefather, the very first Snyman, was coloured.

It's raining now, a soft, light drizzle that clings to my face and shoulders.

I stroll across the yard, past the restaurant, and continue on to the cemetery I'd driven past on my way in. Christoffel's grave should be there.

What did he look like? Burly, like many of the Snyman men? The farmhouse he and Margot lived in is no longer here, and just a section of the original cellar remains. It forms part of the restaurant now.

How Christoffel managed to buy the farm isn't clear. Hans Christoffel Schneider, his father, apparently disappeared from Groot Catrijn's life before the birth of his son. Later she married Antonij Janz from Bengal, a slave who had permission to own land – a so-called free black. Antonij and Groot Catrijn raised Christoffel. Both died around 1682 – it may have been in a smallpox epidemic – so perhaps it was Christoffel's inheritance that enabled him to buy the farm.

Little is certain about Christoffel, apart from the fact that he married Margot around 1690. She was the daughter of Jacques de Savoye and Marie-Madeleine du Pont who arrived at the Cape with the Huguenots in 1688.

The cemetery lies on an open piece of land among the vineyards. It's tidy, and I can see that it has been weeded. The artificial flowers on some of the graves are new and must have been put there fairly recently. Harold Louis Silberbauer, Anna Sybella Schelpe, Gustav Kemp, Josina Klue and Thomas Ellanes Withington all lie buried here. I walk from one grave to the next. Sylvia Elizabeth Bouwer. John Bester. *In tere herinnering.* In loving memory. No Christoffel Snyman.

The slender shadow of a cypress moves on the ground, like an angry pointing finger.

Not one Snyman is buried here. This could be because Christoffel was the only Snyman ever to own the farm. After his death, Margot married Henning Viljoen, and from here on, her and Christoffel's nine children – seven daughters and two sons – spread throughout the country.

As I walk back to the yard, I wonder whether this footpath was here in Christoffel's time. At some time, each of those nine children, the first nine Snymans, must have followed a road away from the farm, whether by foot, on horseback, in a horse cart or ox-wagon, to settle somewhere else. Some, like those on our side of the family, crossed the mountains and moved inland. First to Graaff-Reinet, then with the Great Trek, on to Natal. More children and grandchildren were born, each following his own path, no longer with a wagon and oxen, but by car or train or bus. Much later it was Oupa's turn, then Pa's, and then mine, each of us following his own path, one that began here on the farm of Christoffel, our dark-skinned ancestor, here where the rain is blanketing the vineyards in a haze.

Apart from his signature preserved behind glass, nothing of Christoffel remains on the farm. Not even an old wine barrel with his name carved into the wood.

I cross the yard again and pass the restaurant where an aroma from the kitchen reminds me of bean soup. I hear the pop of a cork as a bottle of wine is opened and then a woman's laugh as if something inside her has been released too.

In Christoffel's time there were elephants here. That first farm-house was probably built from clay. It can't have been a romantic existence. There were clashes with the Huguenot and the Khoi and the San. The Huguenots also disagreed among themselves, yet Christoffel's marriage to Margot wasn't unacceptable, he with his brown skin, she the daughter of Jacques and Marie-Madeleine de Savoye from Aeth in France.

The separate marriages and separate neighbourhoods and separate hospitals and separate schools and separate parks and separate beaches, and the police who enforced the laws to keep everyone separate, only came much later.

I go back inside the museum. Tiaan the guide comes over again. He shakes his head when I ask whether Christoffel is buried here. A team of archaeologists came to the farm to dig, searching for graves and the remains of buildings, but no one was able to find his grave. "But why are you looking for his grave?" He strokes his sparse beard. "Are you writing everything about the Snymans, sir? Then you must talk to oom Koos. He's a Snyman. He lives just over there."

Oom Koos doesn't own the farm. It's jointly owned by a neurologist from Cape Town and a British businessman.

"Oom Koos just works here." Tiaan points towards the cellar. "You drive past the cellar, and then down there, through the vineyards. You'll see the small white houses. The third one is his."

The road to oom Koos's house hasn't been tarred. I drive slowly past a shed. Over towards Franschhoek, the sky is clearing.

Pa should have been here, and so should my late grandpa, for that matter. Oupa loved tracing the family tree, but he never mentioned Christoffel and Groot Catrijn. I doubt if he knew about them.

As far as my oupa and pa were concerned, the Snymans began with great-grandpa Coenraad who went on the Great Trek and fought in the Battle of Blood River.

Then I remember The List. When was that again? Could it have been the eighties? All I can remember is everyone in our town asking one another: "Are you on The List?"

At the time, Dr Hans Heese, a historian, researched the mixed-race population of the Old Cape, and this led to magazine articles and newspaper reports. There was also a list of well-known Afrikaans families that weren't perhaps as pure-blooded and pedigreed as they'd have liked to believe.

The List remained a topic of conversation for a while and then faded away as if it and the issues surrounding it had never existed. The reason we were so certain of who we were was because we couldn't afford to admit where we really came from.

The narrow road lurches deeper into the vineyards before it reaches a row of labourers' cottages on a bare patch. The semi-detached houses remind me of once typical working-class neighbourhoods: row upon row upon row of houses, each with a stoep, a path leading straight to the door, and a silver-painted garden gate.

There's a washing machine on the stoep of the third house. I pull up outside and get out of the bakkie.

At home I have an old black-and-white snapshot of the house my parents lived in years ago in Newcastle, Natal, when Pa was a fitter and turner with Iscor. It was a semi like this.

Three kittens are playing on a blanket next to the washing machine. Next to the front door is a flowering geranium in a paint tin. I knock.

A man opens the door and puts out his hand to greet me. "Good morning, Meneer. I'm Koos Snyman." Oom Koos.

I tell him that I too am a Snyman.

"Grieta!" oom Koos calls down the passage. "Griettt-aaa!"

The sitting-cum-dining room in Ma and Pa's Newcastle semi could easily have looked like this: a colourful couch and chairs with crocheted armrest covers. Sunfilter curtains. A painting of pinkish waves breaking on a pinkish beach.

Somewhere in my garage I have some of Ma's ornaments in a box – ornaments much like the ones on the shelf in this room: a porcelain dog, two egg cups, a small purple vase with a spout.

For years we had a kitchen table just like this, with a melamine top.

"Grieta!" he calls again. "Griettt-aaa!"

A small woman enters the room.

Oom Koos gestures in my direction. "This gentleman's surname is Snyman too."

Tant Grieta's hand goes up to her mouth. "O, jinne, really?" She points to the table with the melamine top. "In that case, Meneer must sit down. We must have coffee." She gestures at the sparkling clean, tidy room. "Please excuse the state of the room. The children always make a mess."

Ma was the same: always making excuses for her spotless home.

Tant Grieta switches on the kettle and oom Koos and I take our seats at the table, me on one side and he on the other. He, the coloured Snyman, and I, the so-called white Snyman; between us, years of heartache and laws and anger and prejudice and misunderstandings.

The conversation starts haltingly – the rain and the work in the vineyards – while tant Grieta takes some mugs from the cupboard. Then oom Koos starts telling me where he was born and the conversation takes off; he stops calling me Meneer.

He was christened Jacobus Abraham Snyman and moved here from Ladismith in the Cape, as a labourer. In 1977.

"They came to fetch us with a lorry. We were at Seekoeigatdrif near Ladismith. With the Bruwers. But they didn't have work for all of us. So a few of us came here, with our things on the back of the lorry." He points to tant Grieta. "She came with."

"We've had our ups and downs," she says, "but we're still here."

Oom Koos's father, Piet, stayed behind in Ladismith. His brother, Hendrik, also came to the Boland at the time.

A young woman enters the room. She's Katrina, one of their daughters.

"He's a Snyman, like us." Oom Koos points to me. "He came for a visit."

Katrina gives me a feeble smile, switches on the television, sits on the couch, and starts watching a repeat of some or other soap opera with the sound off. Their other daughter is called Sara, just like Ma.

Oom Koos has lost track of some of the Snymans on his side of the family. Many have died, and the children and cousins have all gone their own way. "We're all over the place. I know there are still a few in Ladismith."

Tant Grieta puts two mugs of coffee on the table between us, as well as a sugar bowl and a milk jug that's covered by a doily with red beads. "Help yourself." He pushes one of the mugs towards me.

I pour a little milk into my coffee. He pours a little milk into his. "Did the people at the museum up there tell you about me?" he asks. "Every now and then I go to see what they're doing."

I add two spoons of sugar to my coffee. He adds two spoons of sugar to his.

"This farm is where we Snymans come from, you know." He stirs his coffee clockwise. So do I. "It's where our roots are."

Tant Grieta opens the top of the stable door and sunlight and the smell of damp earth fill the room. It's still drizzling outside, but some of the cloud has lifted and a pale sun is shining on the vineyards. Outside, the monkey's wedding continues as the two of us, oom Koos and I, drink our coffee together.

PART II

Into the country

1.

"Let's be honest," says Attie du Plooy as he pushes his can of Stoney ginger beer to one side on the table. "This country is buggered – completely buggered."

I look at him but say nothing. I barely know him.

When I sat down at the table in the Central Café in De Doorns, on the N1 on the other side of Worcester, Attie was already there. He looks around sixty, perhaps a worn-out fifty. His mop of hair sits on his head like the thatched roof of a rondavel. He's drinking a Stoney, and on the table in front of him are a handful of Lotto tickets and a Bic pen that's been chewed white.

At first he wanted to know whether I was on my way to Cape Town, because he was looking for a lift to Kraaifontein. Then a little later, he leaned over and introduced himself: "By the way, I'm Attie."

By then he'd already told me how he'd lost his job on a wine farm here in the Hex Valley, that the owner of the farm apparently owed him R5 000, that his wife and two little girls were with her sister in Rawsonville, and that the bearings on his Opel Kadett had seized.

He'd apparently also applied for a disability grant months ago – he has a leaky heart and trouble with his back – but he hasn't yet heard a word from the Department of Social Development.

He doesn't take his small eyes off me. "I have to beg the government for a pension when there are schoolchildren in the township who get money every month." He drags the Stoney towards himself across the table. "Nice, hey? You make your first baby in standard 7 and the government pays . . . There's a girl – a matric girl! – with three little ones."

It seems the girl is here in De Doorns.

"Here, my friend. *Here*. In De Doorns East. Go and ask over there. I s'pose you know why they have so many children? To get more money from the government! Because the government pays per child."

From the table at the Central Café I have a good view of De Doorns's main street. I can see the Absa building and Pep Stores and a small brown building with a sign that reads *Valley Funerals*. Past it, further up the street, is the co-op.

Across the street, at the Central Garage, a petrol attendant is sitting on an upside-down cooldrink crate. He's holding a cellphone and appears to be SMSing. A clapped-out Mazda bakkie stops in front of Valley Funerals, a man and two women in the cab. There are more people under the canopy in the back. The driver, a little old man wearing heavy black-rimmed glasses with thick lenses, gets out and disappears into Valley Funerals. The others wait in the bakkie.

I can't remember how long it's been since I last sat at a table in a café like this, having a cooldrink and looking out over the street. Few cafés still have tables to sit at. A café isn't a place to relax in any more.

This one looks like a relic from a bygone era. Outside, there's a Coke sign on the gable, and inside, the greyish floor tiles are worn in places. Glass jars with sweets are lined up on the counter: Wilson's toffees, liquorice, apricot sweets. A hand written sign has been stuck on the magazine rack: *No reading*.

The man behind the counter could be Portuguese. "One fish and chips!" he shouts towards the kitchen. "With plenty vinegar!"

At the table next to me, Attie starts getting up in his scuffed, black Bronx shoes. He folds the Lotto tickets in half and puts them in his breast pocket along with the pen. "It's time for me to go. See you. Okay?" He walks off as if we'd never met.

24

I don't know if I'll ever see him again. I'm headed in the opposite direction, north. In all the years I've travelled along the N1, I've never stopped at De Doorns before. This time I decided to stop, even if only for a cooldrink.

The old man comes out of the door at Valley Funerals. He's holding a sheet of paper and looks at it intently as he walks to the bakkie. Could it be a quotation for a funeral? He stops behind the bakkie, lifts the canopy's flap, and talks to the people in the back. Maybe they're from a township or squatter camp nearby and someone close to them has died.

This is grape country, and each year, I hear, hundreds of people, poor and unemployed, come from as far as Zimbabwe to look for work here in the vineyards. Maybe those in the back of the bakkie are people like this, for it has an Eastern Cape number plate.

I'm tempted to ask the man what they're doing here. What's life like for people who go around in a bakkie like that?

Lately it feels as though there are too many things in our country, important things about how people live and die, that I know next to nothing about. I see tired old bakkies full of people, strugglers in scuffed shoes, beggars, queues outside government buildings, and I have no idea what these people's lives are like. It's making me feel like a stranger in my own country.

There are other reasons why the country feels unfamiliar: the murders, the robberies, the potholes in the road and the bullet holes in the road signs – the never-ending news reports of violence and anger and despair from the rural areas.

Sometimes I even feel out of place because of who I am: a white Afrikaner who had a privileged small-town upbringing. I benefited from apartheid and don't know how I should feel about the past. Some people say I should reflect on it, quietly and remorsefully. Others say I don't have to feel so bad about what's in the past, that there are valid reasons for the cruelties and the outrages.

And then there are those, even members of my family, who tell me: forget everything, pack up, put your things on the plane and come with us to Australia or Canada.

Everywhere I come across people, especially on TV and radio, in the newspapers and on the internet and in debating forums, who tell me how I should feel about the country's past or its future. I listen and join in, but there's a time for listening and a time for talking, I've decided, and a time for hitting the road, for heading into the country.

In my bakkie that's parked in front of the café, I have the basics: clothes, a laptop, a camera, notebooks, and a can of pepper spray for self-defence. I want to experience again this country we talk and talk about so much. I want to try and understand for myself what's making me feel like an unwelcome stranger here. I want to try and find out where I fit in.

I want to know if I still belong here.

It looks as if the man with the spectacles and the people in the bakkie outside Valley Funerals have reached a decision. He pushes the sheet of paper into his jacket pocket and slides into the driver's seat. A dark cloud of petrol fumes erupts behind the bakkie when he starts it. I try to count the people in the back when it comes past me, but they're packed too tightly. For a moment the smell of petrol lingers in the street, and then it too is gone.

I drive back towards the N1, which passes the town to the south. To the west the Matroosberg, with one of the highest mountain peaks in the area, is covered in a haze that looks like steam.

Back on the N1, I turn in the direction of Touws River. A little way along, I see the road sign indicating left: De Doorns East.

Only then, once I've taken the turn-off, do I realise what I'm about to do: I'm going to look for the matric girl with the three children Attie mentioned in the café. But what will I do when I find her?

De Doorns East isn't a squatter camp. The brick houses are small and without stoeps, their front gardens bare. In one of the yards an old-fashioned bedpost leans against a wall, and a woman wearing a green headscarf is sitting on a kitchen chair in the front doorway. Perhaps she knows the girl. I pull up in front of the house. It doesn't feel right to turn up at a stranger's house like this to ask strange questions, but what else am I supposed to do?

I've heard that some people, especially antique dealers, often visit townships and go through people's homes in search of furniture to buy. Perhaps I should start by pretending to be interested in the bedpost leaning against the wall.

The woman comes over in her blue slippers. Emily Stuurman. Behind her, on a wall unit in the sitting room, an empty Grünberger Stein bottle stands on display, like an ornament. Tannie Emily's in the mood for a chat.

After we've discussed the bedpost and a few other things, she teaches me a new word: AllPay.

AllPay is an umbrella term for the various social grants paid by the government each month, for children up to fourteen, for people over sixty, and for people with disabilities.

But AllPay also refers to the day, usually at the beginning of the month, when these grants are paid. Then a whole procession of officials and security guards descend on the community hall, because most of the people who get the grants don't have bank accounts. They come to wait in line for cash.

"AllPay is our life," she says, "and AllPay is the cause of some people's troubles."

She was employed in Cape Town as a domestic worker for many years, and now depends on the R1 080 old-age pension she gets from the government each month. She doesn't know of any matric girl with three children around here, but perhaps her sister will. She also lives here, Emily explains as she goes to call her from the Telkom phone in the bedroom.

I wait in the sitting room. On the wall unit below the empty Grünberger Stein bottle stands a television set and several other items: a ceramic dog, a head-and-shoulders photograph in a paper frame of a girl in a school uniform, a torch, a mug that says *Grandma*.

Next to the wall unit is a couch. Although it's no longer new, the cushions are still covered in plastic, just like the day they left the shop.

I listen to tannie Emily's voice coming from the room, and it occurs to me that it's impossible to approach this country as if it's a warm bath on a cold day. There's no way you can prepare yourself for what's coming. Its warm-heartedness is completely overwhelming. One minute you're sitting in the Central Café, and the next you're standing in a stranger's house.

She returns from the bedroom. Her sister doesn't know of a matric girl with three children either. "But she says you must go and ask in Touws River. Tomorrow is their AllPay day."

2.

I head for Touws River, the next town along the N1, to experience an AllPay day for myself. Perhaps there I'll find a young girl who has one or more babies for the extra money.

Isn't this what this country does to us? Force us to think the unthinkable? The child support grant is R250 per child. Would someone really have a child for a mere R250 a month? Or three for R750 a month?

The road climbs the Hex River Mountain, and when you get to the top the landscape changes to Karoo veld: wild rosemary, bluebush, nenta bush; here and there a clump of karee.

The bakkie's radio is tuned to Radio Sonder Grense. The presenter is reading the financial indicators; the American dollar has dipped slightly against the euro and the British pound, but the rand is performing consistently on the markets.

Then my cellphone rings in the nook next to the gear lever. It's Pa, from his cellphone. I pull over. He'd called early that morning too, from his bed. He sounded a little tired then, but his voice is stronger now.

He did get up eventually, he says, and is eating an orange at the kitchen table.

He's in the old house in Ventersdorp, at the table with the oilcloth, the church calendar on the wall behind him. Some oranges, usually with three or four overripe bananas, are in a wooden bowl on the table, next to the portable radio that has a wire coat hanger for an aerial. He always sits on the chair that faces the window, with a newspaper or a magazine close at hand, usually open at the crossword he's busy doing. His pocketknife with the narrow sharpened blade will be there too, with the long unbroken orange peel, because Pa believes an orange should be peeled with a knife, around and around carefully, without nicking the membrane.

"Where are you, son?" he wants to know. "Will you be sleeping in Franschhoek tonight?"

A few days ago I tried to explain to him over the phone what I'm going to do: that I want to drive around the country for a while, without any real plan, that I am tired of feeling out of place in our country. That I want to start where the Snymans' story in South Africa began, on the farm outside Franschhoek. But I don't think he understood much. For him, even on family holidays when I was a child, travel is just a way of reaching a destination. You drive from A to B. And when you've done what you wanted to do at point B, you return to point A.

"I've passed De Doorns already, Pa," I say.

"I thought you said you were going to Franschhoek."

"I've already been there, Pa."

"Why did you go there again?"

It had felt right to start my journey on the farm at Franschhoek. I felt I wanted to say to Christoffel, the first Snyman: "I'm at peace about who Oupa was. Wish me luck for the long road ahead." But I don't tell Pa that. I decide that this isn't the time for discussing Christoffel, our coloured Snyman ancestor, with him. We can talk about it around the kitchen table when I am there with him. So instead, I say: "I just wanted to see what it looked like, Pa. I'll come and show you the photos."

"Do you have somewhere to sleep tonight, son?"

"Maybe in Touws River."

"Touws River? Why Touws River?"

"I'd like to be there tomorrow when the people get their pension money. To see what it's like."

As soon as the words have left my lips I realise it was the wrong thing to say. It sets him off instantly: "If you want to see what it's like, you must come here. Every month there are queues outside the post office as they wait for their pension money. They drink and make a noise and make a mess on the pavements. You should see what it looks like. I don't know what this government is doing ..."

I don't like talking politics with Pa any more. He gets too excited, and his heart is worn out. One of the chambers has calcified and some of the arteries are blocked. He's too weak for an operation. Some days he doesn't even get out of bed. There's nothing the doctors can do, except prescribe more medicine.

Twenty, thirty years ago, Touws River was one of the country's most important railway towns. It used to be known as the place where steam locomotives were brought to be repaired. But the workshop closed for good long ago. Some of the people who used to work there are probably living on AllPay now.

Even the Moedhou Farm Stall just outside town has admitted defeat and closed its doors.

In the main street, opposite the Sonstraal Crèche, I see an ANC poster left over from last year's general election: *W r in tog th r w c n d m e.*

Most of the houses in town are railway houses – railway houses without railway people. For the last few years, Transnet, the old South African Railways, has been selling them to whoever wants one. The country is littered with railway houses like these: red bricks up to the windowsill and then cream-coloured paint up to the roof. Tin roof. Red stoep. Straight garden path. A letterbox with a pitched roof next to a silver garden gate.

I drive down the main road with its Spar, Indraf Café, China shop and the Touws River Pharmacy. I stop and get out. The pharmacy's windows are covered with stickers and posters. It's as if the advertisements reflect the fears and dreams of an entire community: heart problems, ulcers, impotence, obesity, wrinkles and rough skin. Looking for burglar bars for your home? Call Piet's Welding Works. Want a coffee mug with your or your children's photo on it? Call Bertha Bredenhann. Another poster invites Touws Rivier's residents to write down any complaints they have about their town and hand them in here at the pharmacy.

Somewhere, among all of this, almost like a cry for help, is a photocopy of Psalm 23: *The Lord is my Shepherd . . .*

Across the street, a man is leaning against the door frame of a small restaurant that is nameless. He introduces himself as Parker. "Everybody here calls me that." The plastic tables inside are covered with red-and-white tablecloths, and I can hear Abba's "Dancing Queen" playing somewhere in the back.

"Ag no, man, you're a day late," he says. "We had AllPay yesterday. I think it's Laingsburg's turn tomorrow. It's a whole roadshow, you know." He whistles. "You should have been here yesterday. It was chaos as usual." He motions in the direction of the Trans-Karoo Bottle Store further down the road. "They sat there the whole day, drinking."

Parker goes to sit at one of the tables. These conversations usually start off with something specific – the chaos of AllPay day – before drifting off into the doldrums with corrupt politicians and the death penalty that should be reinstated. All the while, you join in the talk, you agree and tell about the time your house was burgled, and as you talk, you know you're repeating hundreds of conversations just like this one, but still you listen and you rage against the government, and, since you're at it, against Julius Malema and his R250 000 Breitling watch.

Parker doesn't know of a matric girl with three children in Touws River. But he does know of a young woman with six children – six welfare children!

"How old is she?"

"I guess about 22, maybe 23."

But he doesn't want to say where her house is. "Find her yourself. I don't want trouble."

The Trans-Karoo was a passenger train that ran between Johannesburg and Cape Town for years, stopping at Touws River on the way. The name of the train has now been changed to the Shosholoza Meyl – but it rarely stops here.

The Trans-Karoo Bottle Store has remained, though, a sad reminder of the train with the same name. There's a notice on the wall:

> NO drunk persons allowed!!!
> NO alcohol on credit!!!
> NO sitting on the tables!!!
> NO alcohol in the toilets!!!

The door is locked. Maybe they're counting their money today.

On the corner, near the pharmacy, there's a low white building with two doors. Above the one, a sign announces in black letters: *Take Aways.* Above the other: *Joepie Fourie Funeral Parlour. Quality service and fair prices.* Inside, an interleading door connects the two.

Maybe Joepie Fourie will know where to find the young mother of six that Parker mentioned. If anyone knows what's what in town, it has to be the undertaker-cum-takeaway owner.

There's no one behind the counter in the half that is the funeral parlour, but there's a certificate on the wall next to the entrance: *New Business Retention 2005. Awarded to Mr J. Fourie.* An old issue of *Men's Health* lies on the desk in the corner.

"Hello!" says a man's voice. "Good mo-o-orning."

A woman comes in from the takeaway side. "Have you been helped?"

"Hello. Good mo-o-orning."

Only then do I spot the African Grey in a cage near the door.

Joepie Fourie isn't here. He died a month ago. On a shelf behind the counter stands a wooden box with his ashes. "Mevrou keeps it there. I guess it'll stay there till she dies, then they'll put it in the coffin with her."

"Hello," says Joepie Fourie's voice. "Good mo-o-orning."

I ask at the office of the ACVV, the Afrikaans Christian women's association, next to the railway line, but Hester Stander, who is in charge today, doesn't know Parker's young woman with the six children.

The ACVV employs a full-time social worker for Touws River, but she's not at the office right now.

"Six children?" Hester asks in disbelief. "I don't know about that."

Schoolgirls with one baby, perhaps two, are another matter. In the Western Cape alone about seven thousand girls between twelve and eighteen fell pregnant in 2010.

The more I ask around town, the more improbable Parker's story sounds. But there's talk of a guy who pretended to have some mental disorder or other, and now gets a disability pension.

Some of the people I ask say they've heard of the young woman with six children, but then refer me to someone else who may be able to tell me exactly who she is and where she lives. Then they, those people who may know, refer me to others who may know. Eventually this brings me to oom Jan Stassen's house in De Beer Street. I've been told he knows everything there is to know in Touws River, but even oom Jan just rests his heavy hands – hands that have punched tickets on the trains for over thirty years – on his silver garden gate and says: "Hell, no, my friend. This is the first I've heard of her."

Oom Jan was a train conductor until the railways forced him to go on early retirement. He looks down the street. "They say you only cry twice here in Touws River," he says, as if that will explain everything. "The day you arrive and the day you leave."

It's dark by the time I leave for Laingsburg – oom Jan agrees that tomorrow is their AllPay day. He knows because his brother-in-law lives there and *he* gets a disability grant.

3.

From a distance, the Lord Milner Hotel looks like a passenger liner that has docked for the evening at Matjiesfontein, on the stretch of N1 between Touws River and Laingsburg.

It's dark by the time I pull up in the parking area outside the hotel. A uniformed porter comes to help me take my things from the bakkie. Yes, he confirms, it's AllPay day in Laingsburg tomorrow. When I ask how he can be sure, he's almost indignant: "They come past here every month, Meneer."

In my room there's a brass bed, and on the bed, two lollipops, one red and one pink. I empty everything I've accumulated in the course of the day from my trouser pockets and put it all on the dressing table: coins, till slips, the wrapper of a Snacker bar. When I'm on the road, more so than when I'm at home, it's a grim battle against chaos, in my head and even in my pockets and luggage.

In my shirt pocket I discover a serviette from Parker's restaurant in Touws River. On it I'd written: *No gathering. No sitting.* I'd seen the words written on the window of one of the shops in the town.

I throw the serviette and the slips in one of Ma's old Tupperware containers – she'd written her name on the lid with pink nail varnish – which I'd brought with me. Then I switch on my laptop and search the internet for statistics on government grants, listening to the whooshing of car and truck tyres on the N1. It sounds like the sea on a stormy night.

The hotel has a shop with a shelf full of second-hand Afrikaans books: Etienne Leroux, Abraham H. de Vries, Opperman, Krog,

Toeks Blignault, Kannemeyer. There's one I'd completely forgotten about: F.A. Venter's *Werfjoernaal*.

In January 1960 my wife, Herman, Elizabeth and I left Johannesburg in a second-hand green Chevy and drove to a farm on the border between Kenhardt and Carnavon to go and live there. The last time I read those words I was at school. *With us, we had Patch, a half-breed cocker spaniel, Pootjies, a half-breed-I-don't-know-what, and Vaaljan, a purebred Siamese.*

I seem to remember seeing an old copy of this book on Pa's bookshelf in Ventersdorp, but I buy it anyway. It's a book I'd like to have on my own shelf; it describes a rural lifestyle I know so well.

The Laird's Arms Pub is near the shop. I walk over. Seated at the counter are two guys: one in a Ferrari jacket he may have bought from a China shop because the seam under the arm has come undone. The other is drinking something that looks like a Bloody Mary.

The hotel was built in 1899 and the bar is an authentic old British pub, complete with a dark wooden counter, wooden floor and piano. I hoist myself onto one of the bar stools and open Venter's book: *After twenty-two years in cities – Johannesburg, Cape Town, Pretoria, Windhoek – we wanted to be farmers and to be free . . .* I struggle to concentrate. The guy in the Ferrari jacket is telling the one with the Bloody Mary about the time he gave a woman and her dog a lift to Worcester. It seems the dog was sick and she wanted to take him to a vet. When they got to Worcester, the dog died in the car.

"I said to her: 'Come, let's throw the dog away.'" The Ferrari jacket's seam opens wider as he gesticulates. "But she said: 'Are you crazy? This dog's going home with me. I'm going to bury him in my own backyard.' So I said to her: 'Hey, I want to do some shopping first, man.' She said: 'Go shop. I'll wait in the car with my dog.' When we got back that afternoon, the dog stank so much you could have got high, my bra."

Next door, in the dining room, a bell rings. Dinnertime.

But first I phone Pa. These days he goes to bed early and I know he'll be wondering if I've found a place to sleep for the night.

He picks up almost immediately: "I was going to call you, son. Have you heard the news? They robbed the bank in Pofadder." Pa's voice is weary, as if the robbery has affected him personally. "Can you believe it, hey? Now they go as far as Pofadder to rob. It's because the police's hands are tied. They do just as they please, these young tsotsis . . ."

They, they, they. Pa with his unrelenting "they".

"You say you feel as if you don't know the country any more. Let me tell you, son, I don't see any hope for us. We're going the same way as the rest of Africa. One of these days we're going to become another Zimbabwe . . ."

I listen to him but don't respond. After a while, I say goodnight and hang up. Even I find it difficult to believe: a robbery at the bank in Pofadder!

The dining room is next to the bar, opposite reception. As I enter, I step into a memory from long ago.

What's happening here is an old-world ritual. One I haven't been part of for a very long time because you don't find old-world hotels like this with dining rooms like this any more. Nowadays small-town hotels are turned into lodges and their dining rooms into steakhouses or à la carte restaurants.

There's a sideboard against one of the walls with an arrangement of dried proteas on it. It stands there like a shrine to good manners. All the tables are covered with white damask tablecloths and all the settings are identical: a sideplate, dinner plate and wine glass. To the left of the dinner plate are two forks, to the right, a knife and a fish knife; above it, a soup spoon and a dessert spoon; all of it, without question, Royal Sheffield silver. A butter knife lies at an angle on the sideplate.

A waiter in a red jacket escorts me to my table and pulls out my chair. *Frans,* says his name tag. All at once it feels as if Pa and my late Ma are with me and the three of us are sitting in the dining room of the Commercial Hotel in Daniëlskuil on a Sunday after church.

A tender feeling of nostalgia descends slowly, like a curtain, over the reality of bank robberies and AllPay days.

First I pick up the stiff, starched napkin perched like a small boat beside the butter knife on the sideplate, unfold it and drape it across my lap – and almost immediately it slips onto the floor. Almost instinctively, my hand reaches out and takes half a slice of white bread from the small plate in the centre of the table. Then I lift the domed lid of the silver dish next to the salt and pepper cellars. Under it lie small ridged butter balls. I know they'll break in half if I press too hard on the butter knife.

Frans returns to the kitchen. The door between the dining room and the kitchen has a silver arm at the top that stops it slamming when a waiter comes in or out with plates in his hands. The mechanism makes a ffft sound as the door closes behind Frans.

A waiter in a black jacket comes over. Freddie. "Something to drink?" He presents me with the wine list in a black cover, bends down to the floor and picks up my napkin, which has slid off my lap again, and hands it to me.

"We'll have the Grünberger Stein," I hear Pa say before he closes the wine list and returns it to the waiter. "And please bring us some ice too."

The typed menu on the table is superfluous. It's impossible to forget. Starters: first soup, then hake. Main course: leg of lamb or chicken with rice, roast potatoes and seasonal vegetables. Dessert: malva pudding and custard.

Frans returns from the kitchen with a soup plate in his hand.

"Ffft," the door whispers behind him.

He puts the vegetable soup with carrot slices floating in it in front of me, and the napkin slides off my lap again.

"Eyes closed," says Ma and takes my hand. "Pa wants to say grace."

"Dear Lord, thank you for watching over us this day," he prays. "We pray that You will protect us this night too. Bless the food we are about to receive and grant that we will never forget Your name. Amen."

4.

In 2011 the government allocated R89 billion for social grants. It cost around R2,4 billion to distribute, and AllPay is the name of the company that helps get the money into people's pockets.

Some 9,8 million women receive a government allowance of R250 per child per month. Some 2,5 million people receive a pension of R1 080 per month. Some 1,2 million people also receive a monthly disability pension of R1 080.

In the dim light of dawn I see these statistics come alive outside the sports grounds near Laingsburg's town centre. This is where the grants are paid out every month. A hundred or so people have already formed a queue. The old man at the front is wearing his church best. The collar of his cream-coloured shirt is threadbare. Lukas Malgas.

Oom Lukas's dreams of what he's going to do with his R1 080 old-age pension aren't big ones. "I just walk around here." He points towards the main street. "By the time I get over there, I won't have much left."

Then the cars and bakkies start pulling up, a procession of deadbeats. One by one, they get out and start putting up tables and displaying all manner of things: frilly dresses and jackets and shoes, blankets and bedding that look as if they're meant to match the dresses. Snoek. Vetkoek. Bright plastic wall clocks made in China. Transistor radios made in China. Nail clippers made in China.

Jerome Cupido is stacking packs of toilet paper. He comes from Paarl, more than a hundred and fifty kilometres away, to sell the toilet paper (R14 for a pack of ten) and duvet sets to the AllPay people here.

A man and a woman pull up in an asthmatic Nissan Sentra. The man takes an enormous loudspeaker from the boot, and before long a mournful voice is wafting through the air: "The earth beneath your feet is holy. Oh, take *off* your shoes. The earth beneath your feet is ho-o-oly . . ." Each month the couple travels from AllPay point to AllPay point to sell the latest CD from gospel singer André Bayman.

An armoured truck and two official Camrys arrive, pass Jerome's toilet paper display, and enter at the gate. The security guards who are here to guard the gates get out of another car. No one will be allowed inside without the proper documents. Eight o'clock. The government's coffers are about to open.

Lukas Malgas is the first to be allowed through the gates, while the queue behind him grows longer and longer. There are girls with babies in their arms and babies on their backs. There's a baby on the back seat of a Mazda 626. There are babies everywhere: on a woman's back, in a girl's arms, in a pram negotiating the gravel on bouncy wheels.

Two men in a not-so-new Mercedes stop near the gate. They don't get out. They wait without opening a window.

I soon realise that two kinds of people gather here. There are the ones at the gate who are getting grant money, and there are those who are here to sell something or who have a claim on the first group's money. Hunter and prey.

Oom Lukas Malgas reappears at the gate in his shirt with the threadbare collar. He takes a R100 note from a brown envelope and looks at it as if it's a mirror showing someone else's reflection. He walks over to a woman on a chair in the shade. She belongs to a burial society that sells funeral policies. Each month she comes to collect money from oom Lukas and her other customers right here.

"Twenty-two rand a month for a hole, a coffin and flowers." Oom Lukas laughs with his mouth but not his eyes.

Now more people are coming out of the gate with their money.

Some go to stand in line at the white Mercedes with the two men still waiting inside. One of the men opens the window a crack, and one by one the people start counting off notes and passing them through the narrow opening.

The men are secretive. One says his name is Wilton Booyse. He sells hampers. "Fifteen kilograms meat, ten kilograms white bread flour and various tins for around five hundred rand," he explains. "I go to buy everything tomorrow, and then it gets delivered to the people here."

It's difficult to fathom exactly how Wilton's business operates. It sounds as if some of the people are still paying off last month's hampers, even though they'll be getting new ones in three days' time. Wilton's brother next to him in the Mercedes runs a cash loan business. For every R100 you borrow, you have to repay R130.

Around me, the town is becoming louder. "Oh, take off your shoes. The earth beneath your feet is ho-o-ly," the loudspeaker next to the Nissan Sentra at the gate has begun singing again, while bedding and toilet rolls change hands and men walk over to the Grand Bottle Store in the main street, which is having a special. Buy a bottle of Old Brown Sherry and stand a chance to win a blanket. Under a pepper tree, a baby boy on a dirty pink bedspread lies with his feet in the air as if he's floating on invisible water. I try to strike up conversations with the young mothers about their babies, but how on earth do you ask, without being rude: "Did you decide to have this baby to get R250 a month?" I don't see a young mother with three or six children anywhere, and wonder whether this isn't the type of myth that speaks of all our fears, a story we tell ourselves to try and give a face to the statistics of poverty? Or a story used by those who have given up, to justify their despair?

5.

Outside Laingsburg, on the N1 on the way to Beaufort West, I see a group of hitchhikers on the left-hand side of the road. I slow down and count them: eight – five men and three women.

The typical hitchhiker who stands next to the road, thumb in the air, is something you don't see much any more. Three of the eight are sitting. One (a woman) is leaning with her back against a white concrete road sign, the other two (men) are sitting on rocks, their feet planted in front of them.

The woman sluggishly lifts a hand, palm upwards, when she spots my bakkie. Not far from her, a young man in jeans with big turn-ups is waving something in the air. Nearly everyone has a neat bag on the ground beside them.

I don't know if this has to do with the spread of cheap Chinese goods throughout the country, but you don't see a hitchhiker with a worn suitcase tied with a belt or a piece of string any more. He – or she – often has a proper travelling bag, sometimes even with a label that says Gucci – genuine fake Gucci.

Eight pairs of eyes watch me as I approach. It's a R10 note the one with the turned-up jeans is waving at me. The woman leaning against the road sign has a bandage around one arm. One of them calls out something, but I can't hear anything through the bakkie's closed windows.

Then they're behind me.

They grow smaller and smaller in my rear-view mirror, an odd picture of wretchedness that settles somewhere in my memory.

We haven't spoken today, Pa and I. When I reach the open road on the other side of Laingsburg, I pull over. The Swartberg Mountains are a dark ridge in the south. I dial Pa's number. His cellphone rings and rings and rings and rings. Then it stops ringing, but the voicemail doesn't come on. For a few moments there's silence, then a shuffle, then I hear him: "Hello . . . Hello." His voice is very soft.

He's been in bed all day, I just know it. When the phone rang on his bedside table he struggled first to find it, and then to find the right button to press.

I picture him on the bed with the imbuia headboard in the room with its pressed ceiling. The bedside table always has more or less the same things arranged on it: a Bible, a flashlight, an old Westclock alarm clock, a can of Old Spice deodorant, a glass for soaking his dentures at night.

"I'm still in bed," he says. "I'm short of breath again today. Where are you?"

"Between Laingsburg and Beaufort West," I say.

"Just remember, I'm with you in that car, son. I'm sitting right next to you. Don't you forget that. But believe me, your pa's had it." Silence. "Where are you going next?"

"I think I'm going to Pofadder, Pa."

"Pofadder? Ag, son, why?"

"I want to see what the bank robbery did to the people."

"When are you coming home? We're waiting for you. It's time you came home."

I don't know how many times I've driven along the N1 without stopping at Prince Albert Road station.

The name can be misleading because Prince Albert Road station is about forty kilometres from Prince Albert. It has a filling station, the North & South Hotel, and a few railway houses on each side of the railway line.

The door and window frames of the station building have been broken, and wasps have made nests in the rooftops. A Camry with a dented right-hand side is resting in front of the North & South.

CY number plates. Bellville. A man is asleep behind the steering wheel, leaning to one side, with the window open and a bottle of Amstel between his legs.

In the bar, at the wide, dark counter, there's one customer, a long, thin, greyish man in Jet Stores denim with a packet of Princeton cigarettes and a bottle of Castle on the counter in front of him.

"What's the deal with the guy in the Camry outside?" He looks at the barman.

"No, I don't know. It was early when he got here and ordered a beer."

"And his car?"

"He says he was hit by a lorry."

"Did he hit the lorry? Or did the lorry hit him?"

"He says it was the lorry that hit him, but I don't know."

"What don't you know?"

"A woman came and asked him for money."

"His wife?"

"No, one of the whores along the road."

This morning's issue of *Die Burger* is lying on the counter:

POFADDER. – The bank in Pofadder has been robbed.

This peaceful Northern Cape community about 170 km east of Springbok was shocked when five men robbed the local FNB branch.

According to Capt. Cherelle Ehlers, a police spokesperson, five men entered the bank at about 15:30. One of the suspects was armed with a .375 Magnum revolver, and another with a knife. They used the weapons to threaten bank personnel but no one was injured. The robbers escaped with an undisclosed sum of money.

The two armed robbers were arrested shortly after the incident and the stolen money was recovered. The three remaining suspects were later arrested near Springbok.

When I go outside again, the man in the Camry is still fast asleep. He's leaning to the left, as if still trying to escape the force of the accident. On the other side of the railway line a number of people have gathered outside a roofless house. Some are pointing to it and others have their hands in front of their mouths. It looks as if the house has just burnt down. The walls are blackened at the top. The windows are missing. Buckled corrugated iron sheets are lying on the ground.

Two children are playing on a rise near the N1. One is pushing a *draadkar;* the other appears to be banging a stone on the ground. I walk over.

It isn't two children. It's a man and a woman. Not so young. Two grown-up children. The man is wearing an old tracksuit; the woman a skirt and a jersey with stretched sleeves.

The man notices me and jogs over, pushing the car in front of him. "B'rrrr'm," he goes, making a sound like a car engine. "B'rrr'mmmm." He turns sharply in front of me and sends the gravel flying from under the wire car's wheels, which are made from old shoe-polish tins. He gives me a toothless smile. "I Attie. Hello." The words sound hollow in his mouth.

The woman is banging two stones against each other and mumbles something I can't quite make out. He points at her. "Poppie."

Attie and Poppie.

They've made paths that crisscross the open space right next to the N1, the two of them have built a whole lot of enclosures made from bricks. In one, a battalion of empty bottles is lined up, waiting. In another, it's a piece of galvanised wire and a rusty sardine tin.

The cars whiz by. Do the people inside them notice us? And what would they see?

"Oupa." Attie points to one of the houses. An elderly man comes out the front door and crosses the empty yard. Klaas Romp. He used to be a labourer on the railways but he's retired now and has been living in Prince Albert Road for years. He's not Attie and Poppie's real grandfather. "They're my wife's sister's children. Their mother died and now they live here with us." He waves his arm to where they're still playing. "They're not well, you see. They were born slow. They play like this every day, there next to the road. Sometimes they understand what you say to them but sometimes they get difficult, especially when they're playing there and I call them home." Silence. "But you know, sir, they're on their own journey. That's all."

Both Attie and Poppie get a monthly disability pension. R1 080 x 2 = R2 160.

The small crowd still hasn't left the burnt-down house on the other side of the railway line. Two men carry a couch out the front door. As soon as they put it down in the yard it collapses on one side.

We stand and watch, Klaas Romp and I, as Attie and his wire car race across the open veld again.

"Yesterday was our AllPay day, you see," says oom Klaas. "A young guy burnt to death in that house."

6.

Between twelve and fifteen million people in South Africa depend on government grants.

7.

Why do I keep thinking of the bank robbery in Pofadder?

At first I thought it was funny: a bank robbery in Pofadder! Ha! Small-dorp drama! Five robbers, a hysterical teller, a flabbergasted police force. Just like an American noir movie, as if Pofadder weren't real and only existed for the sake of the story.

And it's possible that some people – especially city people – do see Pofadder as the prototype of a dorp, rather than an actual dorp. To those people, every backwater miles from the city is a Pofadder.

Daniëlskuil, the little place in the Northern Cape where I grew up, is one of those towns, far from everything and close to itself. Life in these towns isn't idyllic and innocent. They also experience theft and rape, and, yes, sometimes people are even murdered in anger. But a robbery is something else.

A bank robbery is something daring, something calculated, something that happens in the big city with its gangs and syndicates. A bank robber hardly ever lives near the bank he robs. He comes from somewhere else, nameless and faceless, leaving behind fear and uncertainty.

Those five men robbed Pofadder of more than money.

Just past Prince Albert Road station, at Leeu-Gamka, I leave the N1 and turn onto the R353. This is the road to Pofadder, which is about four hundred kilometres north of here, past Fraserburg and Williston, in Bushmanland. If all goes well I'll be sleeping in Brandvlei, in the Brandvlei Hotel, where I met Mozart the tame meerkat on a previous trip.

8.

The Brandvlei Hotel is in Brandvlei's main road. It's a low green building with a wide veranda. *China Store*, I read on the gable of the building next to it. *Clothes, shoes, bags, suitcases, TVs, hi-fis. Very low prices.*

A China shop in Brandvlei? Brandvlei is nowhere near China. It's nowhere near anywhere. It's about three hundred kilometres to Upington in the north, seven hundred to Cape Town in the south.

Brandvlei is one of those dorpies that don't pass the Snacker test. Granted, there may be exceptions, but I've noticed that generally in a really small South African town, you won't find a Snacker on the café shelf along with the Crunchies, the Bar-Ones and the Lunch Bars. You can't buy a Snacker anywhere in these dorps. It's as if the people are still untouched by the pretentiousness of chocolate-covered muesli and sunflower seeds.

Christmas lights decorate the wall of the town council building. Christmas was months ago. Across the street, as in Touws River, an ANC poster from the last election hangs from a lamp post, tattered and faded: *T th r we c d m re.*

It's said the town was named for a man called Brand, one of the trekboere who left the Cape in the 1800s and came to these open spaces in search of freedom and grazing for his cattle.

There's no one behind the reception desk at the hotel. Mozart is nowhere to be seen. Everything in the entrance and the neighbouring lounge bears testament to the hotel's one-star status: the silver bell on the counter, the basket of plastic fruit (one banana and four very red apples) on the table, the low bamboo chairs with their speckled red cushions, the tired Van Dyck carpet where a path has been worn to the door marked *Gents*.

In the bar there's only a young man in a blue tracksuit and he's not the barman. Here, as in so many other bars, a fruit machine has replaced the dartboard against the wall – just one fruit machine that bears a warning in black koki: *Play at own risk*. The young man sits on a bar stool in front of the machine and doesn't take his eyes off the spinning fruit and numbers. "They aren't here," he says, without looking up. "They'll be back just now."

In Daniëlskuil, back in the seventies, we were taught to fear the Chinese. The grown-ups talked about the Red Chinese and how dangerous they were and that they were coming to take our country from us.

At the time, one of the trivia questions on Chappies bubblegum wrappers was: *Did you know? If all the Chinese in the world were to jump one foot into the air at the same time, the earth would be knocked from its orbit when they landed.* That had us rather worried. What if the Chinese decided to jump?

Now Brandvlei has a China shop, just like countless other South African towns. These China shops hardly ever close, not even at Christmas. I go in. Radios, heaters, fans and other electronic goods are stacked on shelves against one wall. The rest of the shop is filled with clothes and shoes. Behind the counter, a Chinese couple are watching a Chinese movie on a small television set. "Hello," says the man with a smile.

They can't speak English or Afrikaans.

"Only China," the man says.

"Only China," the woman confirms.

"It's hard to hammer anything into them, Meneer," a woman's voice says behind me. "They come straight from China, these two. But we've managed to teach them to say 'baie dankie' – 'thank you'."

The voice belongs to Fytjie de Wee who works at the Voorsorg Café next door. She struggles to pronounce their names. "He is Chin and she is Sjjj . . ." Her tongue's twisted. "Come, let's ask Mrs Coetzee. She's next door. She knows."

"Baie dankie," Chin says as we leave.

"Baie dankie," echoes the small woman.

Monica Coetzee is sitting on a chair behind the till in the Voorsorg Café. In addition to a Bafana sausage roll and cooldrink, you can also buy a small funeral wreath here. Monica also struggles to pronounce the woman's name, but it sounds as if it could be Zhal. "They came here about four months ago," she says. "Before, there was another Chinese, Wayne. He started the shop. He stayed here for four years, easy. These two arrived when he left."

Neither Monica nor Fytjie knows exactly how this Wayne heard of Brandvlei or why he decided to open a store here.

Chin and Zhal live in a small flat at the back of the shop. Sometimes they go off in their panel van and return a day or two later with a load of new supplies – more cheap clothes and goods.

"Except for that, they never leave the shop," says Monica. "They don't go anywhere in town because they don't understand anything. It must be terrible. If I think how trapped I sometimes feel, sitting here for eight hours a day, I can't imagine how they must feel."

They do sometimes come to buy something from the café – mainly chicken or cabbage or potatoes.

Fytjie moves a little closer. "Yesterday, the man came in here and started making funny signs." She makes wave-like motions with her hands in the air. "At first I thought: is he looking for a snake? Where are we going to get him a snake? Then I realised, no, he's looking for fish."

"But they're Christians," Monica interrupts. "The woman came here to show us her Bible. I believe they practise their faith in their own way."

"But it's not easy to work for them," Fytjie retorts. "They don't like to pay."

Fytjie walks to the door. "They've also shown us their house in China. The pictures are on their computer. Would you like me to show you?"

We walk out of the café and into the China Store. Chin and Zhal are still staring at the television screen.

"This man wants to see your house over there in China." Fytjie points to me but Chin just stares at us as if the narrow counter is an ocean dividing us.

"On your laptop. Show him your house on your laptop."

"Laptop?"

"Show us your house – your house! On your computer."

Chin looks as if he understood this time because he takes out a laptop and switches it on. He taps at some keys and then turns it towards us. On the screen is a picture of a small Chinese woman with a rice paddy in the background. "Mamma," he says. "Mamma."

"It's his mother." Fytjie leans over to get a closer look. "Shame."

Fytjie comes with me when I leave. There's something she wants to tell me: "They sometimes come to our house. They just show up but not to visit. They come to play with my children. They and the children play with a ball and laugh, and when they've had enough, they say goodbye and drive off in the van."

This time there's someone behind the reception desk at the hotel. Billy Fourie. He's the manager at the hotel because the owner, Alan Greeff, has moved to Christiana.

The last time I was here, Alan still ran the hotel. The meerkat belonged to him and followed him everywhere in the hotel. He'd felt sorry for the little creature and bought it for R30 or something like that from a drunk outside the bottle store.

Above the bed in my room, attached to the wall, is an old hotel radio, one that looks like a box with rectangular white switches marked: *Afrikaans, English, Regional.* I push them, but nothing happens.

There's a white peppermint in a cellophane wrapper on the bed.

I try reading F.A. Venter again but keep returning to the same paragraph: *The country worms its way into your soul. It's something subtle, invisible and intangible, a silent shaping of the heart*

and senses, like the spirit of a child in its parents' home. He be-
comes a father to you, a father who disciplines you, but against
whom you will never revolt, who may even hurt you, but whom
you will never abandon. He has made everyone here his children
and that's why they are one, that's why they live in a laager.

There's a noise in the street. Two men are fighting outside the
bottle store. One is wearing a long-sleeved brown army shirt someone probably gave him. The breast pocket is torn, the buttonless
epaulettes bounce up and down as he swears and screams at the
other man who is bleeding from the side of his head as he's led
away by two younger men.

The gambler in the tracksuit is peering out of the bar window.

Chin comes out of the China shop and walks over to the hotel.
A handful of gangly boys pass by. One shouts, "Ching, chong, cha!"
while the others giggle. "Ching, chong, cha!"

"Baie dankie," Chin smiles at them. "Baie dankie."

Later that evening, I ask Billy Fourie what became of Mozart the
meerkat.

"Someone kicked old Mozzie to death, one of the guests. I don't
know whether he got a fright. The man was sitting in the dining
room and when Mozzie walked in, he jumped up and kicked old
Mozzie, and he died."

Pottie Potgieter still can't believe that it really happened, here, in
Pofadder. Here, where he's owned the Shell garage in the main road
for more than twenty years, and where there's never been anything
but peace and quiet. "Can you believe it, old pal? A bloody robbery.
Here."

He's standing on the pavement outside the garage and points to
the small turquoise-and-white First National Bank Building past
the Boesmanland Café. It's just after eight, and Pep Stores across
the road isn't open yet.

"I went over there as soon as I heard." Pottie points down the road
again. "I wanted to check they didn't get my savings." But when he

got there, the police had already caught one of the robbers. "Apparently he said to the policeman: 'Sorry, sir. We tried, but we failed.'"

A Nissan Sentra comes towards us from the top of the street, from the direction of the Sophia Old-Age Home. "Here comes the young woman who works at the bank," says Pottie. "She's the one who had the gun against her head."

Pottie walks into the road and puts up his hand. The Sentra stops. Behind the steering wheel is a youngish woman wearing a bank uniform with a gold name tag: Daphne Herbst. They greet each other and Pottie points to me. "Come and tell this man what happened," he says.

"I'm sorry, Oom," she replies. "I'm not allowed to talk about it."

"They mos held the gun to your head?" asks Pottie.

"Yes, Oom, they did."

"And you lay on the floor?"

"Yes, Oom."

"And you were shaking with shock?"

"Yes, Oom."

"And then someone called the police?"

"Yes, Oom."

Pottie gives me a bag of droëwors and biltong before I continue on my way to the bank. The pavements are clean and tidy. In a side street I see a team of workers filling the cracks in the road with tar.

One of the workers comes over. Edward Cloete. "The people in Pofadder talk a lot of nonsense. There were seven robbers. They came in two Hondas."

"I thought they said it was a Quantum minibus?" one of his colleagues cuts him short.

"It was two Hondas. A white one and a blue one." He points to the back of the post office next to the bank. "We found the one crook there. He was lying on the ground, trying to break his cellphone with his hands."

Almost everywhere I go, the people of Pofadder are discussing the robbery, using words that subtly, invisibly, intangibly spread among them, sounding different to different ears until no one can say with certainty if it was five or seven men, if it was a Honda car or a Quantum minibus.

At his house next to the Sophia Old-Age Home, oom Koos Louw, a former member of the old provincial council, isn't keen to discuss the robbery. He doesn't have all the facts. "You have to speak to Gertjie Niemoller," he says. "Gertjie lives opposite the bank."

But first I pop in at the police station. Captain Patrick Mojo, the station commissioner, has maps of the area pinned up in his office. He puts his elbows on his desk and sketches the situation as the police have it: five men were arrested for the robbery, and all five are from Khayelitsha in Cape Town. They arrived in a Quantum minibus. Two apparently entered the building while a third waited outside near the church and the other two waited in the minibus. Daphne Herbst was talking to someone at First National Bank's branch in Kakamas when the two robbers entered the bank. There were no clients in the bank. Someone from the branch in Kakamas phoned captain Mojo's team and they responded immediately.

A bag full of money was recovered, but Captain Mojo doesn't want to say how much it was. Some say there was R12 000 inside the bag, others say it was R150 000 – and that one of the robbers jumped into a corrugated-iron dam with the bag.

Oom Gertjie Niemoller owns the whole block opposite the bank. He could, for all I know, own most of Pofadder, because just about everyone tells me he's a wealthy man. That he's owned more than one mine in his day, that he farmed with fifteen thousand karakul, that he started South Africa's date industry. And that he's the only person from Bushmanland who has flown in a Concorde.

That may be so, but his yard doesn't speak of wealth. A Kombi is parked under a lean-to, and there's a small cement dam where he keeps the turtle he bought in Pretoria in 1953. No Italian tiles. No water fountains.

A man peeps out of a side door. He's wearing a blue overall jacket and velskoene – this is the closest you'll get to a Bushmanland butler. Marsie is his name. Marsie Silo. "He's just finished showering," says Marsie. "Please come in."

Marsie walks ahead and escorts me to a huge rectangular room. Against one wall is a long bookshelf and a cupboard with documents stacked on top. A shoebox full of stones sits on a table. An empty birdcage stands to one side. On the desk, two ashtrays, a pair of binoculars, a packet of Prohep, a tattered cheque book, an ice-cream container full of paperclips, and behind the desk, oom Gertjie in a cream safari suit.

"I hope things are going well, Oom?"

"No, man. I don't have much longer left. I mean, I'm eighty-two – and I haven't taken care of my body. I smoked and drank, otherwise I might have made it to ninety." He stares dejectedly at his legs. "It's difficult to walk. So now I just sit here."

Oom Gertijie's workers told him about the robbery across the street. "It's no joke the way they're stealing and robbing in this country." He opens a drawer and takes something out: a gas pistol. He used it once on a man who came here and annoyed him. He points to the red stains on the walls and ceiling. "I didn't know this thing could shoot like that. The man came here, I don't know whether he wanted to steal or what. But he was aggressive. I said to him: 'Go away.' But he kept wanting to come in here." Oom Gertjie points the gas pistol in the air. "So I took this thing and pulled the trigger, and it just started spraying. The guy was in such a hurry to get away that he left one of his shoes behind in the yard."

Not that oom Gertjie likes violence. On his date farm he had a never-ending problem with baboons eating the dates. "Eventually, I took an old car tyre and cut it in half. Then I filled it with wine and put it in the veld. Man, you should have seen the baboons. They had a great time. Soon the whole lot of them passed out around the tyre. Then I took my gun and went right up to them. But I couldn't bring myself to shoot them."

Oom Gertjie used to own four Tretchikoff originals but over time too many people came to hear about them. "People would just turn up – strangers. They'd come from the city and get out of their cars and say: 'Oom, are you the one with the Tretchikoffs?' And then they'd walk through the house."

So he decided to sell the Tretchikoffs for a good price. "Otherwise someone probably would have stolen them too."

A security guard is on duty outside the bank opposite oom Gertjie's house. He stands close to the autobank with a machine gun slung over his shoulder. Every now and then he looks at his cellphone screen.

In the hotel a little further up the road, oom Faan Burger, someone else who has lived here for years, comes into the bar while I'm there. "Can I tell you something?" He looks at the barman.

"Yes, sir, if you like."

"I prayed for you last night."

Oom Faan turns to me. "I pray for coloured people too. And they pray for us. In this town, we all pray for one another. And why not? What's wrong with that?"

9.

Just after eight the next morning, I'm still in my room in the Pofadder Hotel when a phone call from Pa wakes me. He sounds much better than yesterday. The doctor says that's how it is with the kind of heart problem he has: up and down, up an down, one last bumpy road between bed and kitchen table.

"I've been sitting in the kitchen for hours," says Pa. "Johannes is making us putu pap."

Johannes Bogotsi began working for Pa as a gardener seven years ago, but now he makes Pa's porridge and rubs Pa's numb feet with homeopathic ointment, puts on Pa's shoes, and ties his laces; and on bad days, when Pa can barely walk, he helps Pa down the passage to the toilet, closes the door, and reappears with Pa a little later.

"Are you still in Pofadder, son?" In the background the sound of Johannes putting the lid on the pot on the stove. "We wish you were here."

There's a hesitation in Pa's voice that's difficult to describe – a hesitation that means something I'm doing or have done is bothering him. If your father has been your father for more than forty years, you pick these things up almost intuitively. "I'm still in Pofadder, yes," I reply.

"I'm worried about you," I hear him say. "Are you all right, son?"

Immediately I'm annoyed. I sit up in the hotel's narrow single bed. On the bedside table is Venter's *Werfjoernaal*, which I finished after midnight last night. "You don't need to worry, Pa," I say. "I'm all right."

"But I do worry about you, son."

"You don't need to, Pa," I repeat as calmly as possible while thinking: you worry about me? How dare you? I'm the one who grapples with the country's problems. I'm the one driving around and wondering on behalf of all of us whether we still have a place here. It's you, Pa, who has given up, blaming the government for everything. You're the one who talks about "them". Shouldn't I be the one to worry, Pa?

In the background I hear the sound of the lid on the pot again.

"It's these youngsters." Every now and then I can almost hear the feisty Pa of old in his voice. "Malema's people – they're the ones making trouble."

"What do you mean, Pa?"

"It's them who robbed that bank. They sit in the townships and do nothing. Most of them can't even read or write properly."

"Maybe the old regime is to blame for the fact they can't read or write properly. The National Party that you voted for all those years."

That was exactly what I didn't want to say, because it just brought on the same passionate lecture about how we still wouldn't have tarred roads and dams and hospitals and clinics in this country if it wasn't for the old government. How it would still be a wilderness.

When he's done, Pa sounds old and worn out again. "I think I'm just quickly going to eat something," he says before saying goodbye, "then I'm going to lie down again."

After breakfast, consisting of the Boesmanland Café's famous Moerse Burger (as stated on the menu), I take the dirt road to Van Wyksvlei, past places with names such as Katkop, Geelvloer and Onderstedorings. I want to go to Constantia, the farm near Van Wyksvlei that F.A. Venter wrote about.

The story moved me for one reason in particular – the innocence of life in the platteland as Venter describes it. It could just as well have been a description of Daniëlskuil and its surroundings in the seventies. It's a bygone farmers' paradise of church bazaars, Sunday school picnics and jovial auctions. The conflicts we knew then were mostly between man and nature: droughts, locusts, diseases that killed sheep and chickens. Granted, politics did exist, but it was the safe politics of Nat versus Sap, of Reformed against Dutch Reformed, of a Ford man and a Chev man. The labourers' houses were set at a distance from the farmer's house, the "location" out of sight of the dorp, and the inhabitants of those houses were good-natured and submissive.

Could it be that I'm only now losing that old innocence? The thought keeps returning as I read. Could this be the first time I'm really noticing the small houses out there on the empty veld?

The world is flat and bare between Pofadder, Brandvlei and Van Wyksvlei.

A small bakkie shudders towards me. A Datsun 1400 with one blue mudguard and one green. The bonnet is tied down with a piece of wire, the left front wheel wobbles over the gravel, the windscreen is a road map of cracks, and inside are a man, a boy and a woman. Another five or six people are on the back. The three inside the cab wave at me. I hear a voice in the wind. Then it's just me and my thoughts again for kilometres through dry river beds, past blackened rocks clustered as if gathered for a meeting.

Between nowhere and nothing I see a dead jackal draped over a wire fence. It's something you see from time to time in this part of the world. Jackals catch sheep, the farmers find them, kill them and hang them on a fence. This one has been here for a couple of days. His front legs are grey and his tongue lolls from an open mouth.

Die Noordwester, a community newspaper I bought in Brandvlei, reports on a jackal that also ended up somewhere on a wire fence.

PRIESKA. – Last week, on her way to the farm school where she is a relief teacher, Sarah Badenhorst saw a jackal running next to the road. At first she took it for a dog, but then realised to her surprise that it was a big jackal.

She immediately swerved off the road, chased the jackal in her bakkie, and drove over a large bush before hitting it. At first, she wasn't sure whether she had hit it but when she looked in her rear-view mirror, she saw the jackal lying in the road. She had to turn back, with half the bush still stuck under the bakkie, to check that it was dead.

It was indeed dead, and they hung it on the wire fence. She later saw a flock of sheep with their lambs not far away – the jackal may have been on its way to them.

After a while I see a greenish hue in the distance and then a blue-gum tree rises from the plain. Swartkop. The Timbuktu of South Africa, I'd thought the only other time I was here, long ago. It has a church, a school, one shop and a few flat-roofed houses. And around two hundred residents.

I spot something red in the veld. I drive through the veld towards it because there aren't many roads here. When I get closer, I realise it's a fire hydrant – one that's filled with chemical powder and used in big buildings in the city, in a red steel cabinet with key behind a glass window. It's hanging there on a pole in the veld like an alien space ship that's landed there.

A fire hydrant in Swartkop? Where not a single house has running water or electricity? Where cellphone reception doesn't exist, and most people use a bicycle or a donkey cart when they want to go somewhere?

Not far from the fire hydrant, a woman comes out of a yard that's been swept clean, her wobbly legs in velskoene, a long pair of men's socks pulled up to her knees. Tannie Sophie Cloete.

"Good morning. And *this*, Tannie?" I put my hand on the fire hydrant.

"It's a fire sprayer, my boy. Three men came and put it here last week."

The sand around the pole that the fire hydrant is attached to is still a little loose.

"Are you afraid there'll be a fire here?

"Ag, this old place will never burn. Never has and never will. See for yourself, we don't even have grass here."

"So why is this thing here then?"

"I honestly don't know, my boy."

Some children saunter over. A barefoot boy starts fiddling with the red box. "Get away from there!" shouts tannie Sophie. "Get away from there!"

She says someone called Jakob Pieterse, who also lives in town, knows how the fire hydrant works but he's not here right now. It seems he also has a fire suit that was given to him by the people who came to install the hydrant.

Tannie Sophie looks towards the school. "Over there's another two. The same."

Could it be some bureaucratic slip-up that's the reason for these hydrants being here? Or is it a case of misplaced service delivery, or a kind of backveld open-toilet saga?

Even before I've reached the school I spot the red box on the pole – the earth around it is also loose. There are three houses and a long-drop nearby, but the fire hydrant is closer to the toilet than to the houses.

The school is closed for the holidays and the doors are locked, but I find a young woman sitting on the steps outside one of the classrooms. Lynette Cloete. Tannie Sophie is her aunt, and Lynette more or less confirms what she's just told me: three men arrived in a silver bakkie and planted the fire hydrants. Then, after speaking to Jakob Pieterse and giving him a fire suit, they disappeared again without showing anyone how they work.

A politician or an official should at the very least have made a speech before officially handing over the fire hydrants to the community. Jakob Pieterse, who seems to be the fire-engineless local fireman, could even have given a demonstration in his brand-new gleaming protective suit.

Oom Piet Titus's house looks as if it had risen out of the ground long, long ago: the walls and the floor are the same dark brown as the earth around it. As one of the oldest inhabitants of Swartkop, oom Piet would know about the fire hydrants.

A donkey cart is standing in front of his house, and under it a skinny dog is lying like a question mark on the ground. Oom Piet's wife, tant Grieta, comes out to meet me. "Come in, my boy. Piet is resting a little. He's not well."

Oom Piet is lying on his back on some bedding on the floor. A patchwork quilt is covering him and there's a torch and a bottle of Borstol next to him. Poverty has long been an invisible lodger in their home. The chair against the wall has a bent leg, the wash-basin is missing a handle, and the transistor radio has a coat hanger for an aerial, just like Pa's on the kitchen table.

His small hand is gnarled and cold. "It's this sickness, you know. I think I'll stay in bed today."

"He'll be in bed tomorrow, too," Tant Grieta sighs. "He's finished."

Oom Piet knows the old, old stories of the area: how they looked for water, herded sheep, and where each donkey is buried. The last time I was here he told me why a puff adder snores at night.

Once he is gone, the stories will be gone too.

Tant Grieta says she saw the bakkie and the men who brought the fire hydrants and how they planted them, but she doesn't know why or wherefore either. Nobody has been over to tell them anything.

At the shop, Magda Maritz, the owner, says the man who brought the fire hydrants was only doing his job. He got a government contract to install fire hydrants in the townships in several Northern Cape towns, but why he came here, she can't say either. The decision was made in a boardroom or an office somewhere far from here.

The result is that Swartkop has four fire hydrants as a tribute of sorts to the strange decisions politicians sometimes make.

10.

It's not hard to find the shop in Van Wyksvlei. Pass the only co-op and carry on until you reach the only hotel and the only butchery. The shop is opposite the butchery.

In Pofadder, Pottie Potgieter told me to ask tannie Breggie Bothma if I wanted to know anything about this area; she would know the directions to the farm that used to belong to F.A. Venter.

I park outside the shop. My cellphone beeps. "You have one voice message," says the voice. There's no reception between Swartkop and Van Wyksvlei. I listen to the voicemail. "Please call when you have a minute," says Pa in a hesitant, almost self-pitying voice. I get out of the bakkie. I'll call him later. The shop smells of everything: mealie-meal and soap and long-forgotten conversations. Behind the wide counter a woman is counting out toffees from a glass jar for two small boys. Tant Breggie.

She must be the oldest shop assistant in South Africa. At eighty-four, she still works full time, week in and week out. "Why would I just go and sit? What would become of me?"

She'd known F.A. Venter when he lived here. Venter's parents had farmed here too. "His father was called Herman and his mother was . . ." Her hand reaches for her mouth in astonishment. "Oh jinne, I've forgotten . . ."

Tannie Max Visser, who works at the butchery across the road, enters the shop.

"Max!" tant Breggie calls to her. "What was Frans Venter's mother's name again?"

"Aunt Nellie."

"That's right. Aunt Nellie. Didn't she die in Kimberley?"

"No, she died here in Van Wyksvlei."

"Now why would I think it was Kimberley?"

"I don't know where you get that idea. I swear she died here."

As for the whereabouts of Constantia, tant Breggie can tell me that with more certainty. "You turn right just down the road here, then you take the Kenhardt road. The first farm you get to is Noute. Carry on, over a small rise. The road veers off like this . . ."

At this point oom Philip de Bruyn joins us. He's a tall, strong man with a Parker Pen and a spectacle case in the breast pocket of his khaki shirt. He also knew Venter. "Frans was a Sap, you know," he says. "Some ignorant guy or other once proposed him as a member of the Rapportryers. But Frans was turned down. A Sap couldn't become a Rapportryer." And then, with a hint of a smile: "I wasn't a Rapportryer either, because I was also a Sap." He looks at me as if he feels sorry for me. "I don't think you'll be able to go to Constantia. It belongs to Armscor now."

Not far from the shop is a disused children's playground, but the fence is gone. All that's left is a section of the slide and the frame that the swings hung from, standing there a bit like the gallows in a cowboy movie.

The only thing that hasn't been damaged is the signpost:

> Use of equipment at your own risk.
> No children over 15 allowed on playground equipment.
> Children under 7 must be accompanied by a competent person.
> No bicycles permitted inside the playground.
> Keys obtainable from the SA Police.
>   – BY ORDER

I pull over on the pavement next to the signpost and call Pa from the bakkie. He must be in his bedroom again because the phone rings and rings, then silence, then there's a scraping and scratching before I hear him: "Hello . . . Hello."

"You called," I say. "Are you all right?"

"Pa's just lying down for a bit," he says.

It's an old trick of his: when he's feeling unwell or sorry for himself, he refers to himself in the third person. "Pa's just lying down for a bit." Silence. "I didn't want to argue with you this morning, but you have to stop thinking that us whites have only been bad for the country."

"That's not what I'm doing, Pa." I'd like to add: "But I can't pretend the bad things never happened." Instead, I keep quiet.

There's a long silence. I look at the sign in front of me. Pa's generation liked putting up notices like these for the sake of law and order. (Always with a "By Order" at the end.) In some places, like here, the noticeboard is all that remains.

"When can we expect to see you?" he asks. "When are you coming home? I worry about you, son."

This is typical too: first he'll admonish, then apologise, and then he'll make me feel like the prodigal son.

I explain that I expect to be in Ventersdorp in a week or two. I haven't experienced enough of the country yet.

"That's all right, son," he says. "As you please. You know better."

"I don't think I always know better, Pa."

"No, you always know better, son."

"That's not true, Pa."

"All I'm saying is, stop making out that us whites were bad all the time. Why don't you go and look at the poor whites living in squatter camps? Is apartheid to blame for that too?"

"I'm not saying the whites were all bad, Pa, but apartheid didn't just happen. You belonged to the Broederbond. You should know, Pa ..."

Then he said some more things and I said some more things, angry things I didn't know I still had in me.

The road to Kenhardt, like most of the dirt roads in Bushmanland, hasn't been graded for a while. I pass Noute and then another farm, but I can't find tant Breggie's "road that veers off like this".

Further along, I see a sign: Breekkierie. It rings a bell, and then it all comes to me; Venter mentioned Breekkierie in the book: *In those days, oom Fras and his wife, tant Meraai, lived on the old farm Breekkierie. Oom Fras was uneasy at Breekkierie because an aunt of his was buried there, and they'd built a small house on her grave. He was convinced this aunt sometimes wandered about the farm ...*

Oom Fras – short for Lafras – was one of the so-called faint-hearted Moolmans so many stories mention. At one time, it's said, oom Fras was riding through Bushmanland on his horse when he started to feel scared, so scared that he got off the horse and crawled behind it on hands and knees to fool the ghosts into thinking he was its foal.

People around here also tell of a man – perhaps he was a Moolman too – who, after going to bed one night, was too scared to get up again to blow out the candle. In the end, he threw a shoe at the candle on the dresser to put it out.

Around here, we like to talk. In the course of our conversations we repeat fairy tales, stories and legends; we take the old, old jewels from the chest, polish them, and pass them around to keep them alive.

Constantia can't be too far from Breekkierie. I see another signpost: Gert and Rossie van Wyk. De Hoop. I decide to turn in. I don't want to get any more lost; I already don't know where I am.

The farmhouse is surrounded by trees. In this part of the world all farmyards look more or less the same. Or could it just be that every old farmyard looks vaguely familiar to me? They all have a windmill and, not too far off, a corrugated-iron dam with lime-encrusted seams. An old bakkie is parked under a pepper tree, and the house is fenced. The yard is swept clean and there's a quiver tree and a rockery. On the veranda wall there's a flowering geranium in an asbestos container, and a fern in a paint tin. On the top step a wire basket sits on a folded grainbag. To the side of the house stands a ridged aluminium tank with a small lock on the tap, to collect rain water. At the back door there's a car radiator for wiping your feet, which has been worn smooth over the years. When you stop and get out, a sheepdog, its back hunched, trots over to the gate, and the screen door under the yellow lightbulb on the stoep squeaks open ...

Rossie van Wyk comes over. She knows Constantia. She points towards two flat-topped hills in the distance. "Venter's house is between those two hills, but I don't know whether you'll be able to go there. The gates are locked."

Venter, who died at the Strand in 1997, sold Constantia before his death to someone who sold it to Armscor. Now Constantia has lost its innocence because it's part of the Alkantpan Test Range.

A narrow two-track lane lurches towards the two hills. It gradually becomes fainter and the Bushmangrass and thornbushes grow higher, before you reach a locked gate. Behind it, in the veld, is the skeleton of a house. Luckily, no one seems to be testing weapons today.

We came from the city and we were like the city – disciplined, hurried and bound by ruthless regulations. On the way to the farm we even sang "California, here we come!" because we were filled with a wild expectation of freedom, space and that undefined romance the veld and its animals evoke in city folk.

Venter helped build this house. I walk up to the gate. A sign cautions *Danger/Gevaar.*

I've never lived on a farm, but somewhere inside me I sometimes feel there's a farm – and not just one. The farm in me is all the farms I've come across and got to know and learnt to love in my life. The farms in history books – farms where homes were burnt down – also help make up my farm. So does this farm.

I climb over the gate and walk across the piece of land that Venter tried to capture in words.

I can see from a distance that the roof, window frames and door frames have been removed. To one side I see a donkey where water used to be heated in a large drum, and behind it, a kennel. Could this have been Patch's kennel?

Patch was the mongrel the Venters brought to the farm. Venter also mentions Antonius and Cleopatra, two swallows that nested under their roof. And dung beetles and termites. And droughts and thunderstorms.

This land is like a mother with a large family and little money. She never gives everything at once. Therefore we very rarely have anything in abundance.

The yard has a quiver tree, but it's otherwise overgrown and missing its silver gate. A rusty corner post is all that remains of the fence around the house, and there isn't a swallow or a typewriter to be heard.

In the open, some distance from the house, there are two roofless labourers' houses among the thorn trees and the skaapbossies.

Venter suffered from very low blood pressure, among other things. There wasn't a doctor nearby and that's why they eventually moved away.

An abandoned house dies quietly and slowly. First the plaster pulls away at the top of the walls and the ants tunnel away in the corners. An aardvark may burrow into one of the rooms, and a thornbush may struggle through a crack in the floor before branching out.

And then, one day, perhaps a thunderstorm will come and the wind will be strong enough to topple one of the walls. Then a second will fall, and then another, and another. And more winds will blow and more rain will fall.

Is that why we feel a little sad whenever we see the ruin of a farmyard next to the road? Is it because we feel as if the farm inside of us is also changing? As if the life we've known ever since we can remember is disappearing?

11.

Sampie Cloete is bent over his Volkswagen Golf at the Engen garage on Carnarvon's main street. "Luckily there isn't too much wrong with her." He peers into the engine. "I just have to take the top off. Something's not right with the valves. Maybe I should get new plug wires too. And plugs. And points." He smiles bravely. "At least her coil still works like a bomb."

Minutes ago he counted out R187,50 in crumpled notes and coins on the roof of the Golf and gave it to the petrol attendant. After putting in a pint of oil and fiddling with the plug wires, the Golf is ready to tackle the long road to Loxton again.

Sampie works at a tyre shop in Calvinia and he and his wife, Melba, and a few of his family members are on their way to Melba's brother's funeral. One by one, the passengers return from the café, all five of them. "Move up, man!" one of the women shouts at the other three on the back seat; then slowly, squeezing to get her leg into the car, she closes the door.

"Well, I must be off." Sampie lowers himself into the driver's seat. Next to him, Melba sips a can of Iron Brew and a fluffy dog with a red bow around its neck hangs from the rear-view mirror. Sampie turns the key. The engine hoi-hois sluggishly, and then there's a bang as it starts and dark fumes come bubbling out of the exhaust. There is a small green sticker in the rear window: Addo Elephant Park. Sampie gives me a thumbs-up and they're off.

They're going to be in time for the funeral wake tonight, all night, in Loxton.

I spent the night in Williston, the neighbouring town, and now

I'm heading in the general direction of Vosburg. As soon as I saw Sampie's Golf, it formed a snapshot in my mind. Perhaps I'm imagining it, but there seem to be more crocks on the road in the Northern Cape than anywhere else in the country. Golfs like Sampie's, Datsun bakkies, Mazda 323s, Chev 4.1s from the seventies.

Perhaps there are more poor people here who need to own cars; the distances between places here are vast, and there's no public transport to speak of.

In the garage café a list with the names of those who are no longer welcome hangs from a shelf. There are no direct accusations, but I gather that theft earns you a spot.

Lately I've seen similar lists in many cafés around here, often written with a koki pen on a piece of cardboard, listing the names of people who aren't welcome.

I've copied the one in the Jaagvlakte Café in Calvinia verbatim into my notebook:

RIGHT OF ADMISSION RESERVED

The following people are prohibited from entering the shop again:
Beuhlah Julius (10) – Hooty Fruit ice cream
Nicolene Ockthuys (13) – ran away from sister
Charmaine Prins (13)
Marsalyn Ambrose (14)
Santie-Ann Ockthuys (The Leader)

BY ORDER
THE OWNER

I'm beginning to think I'm not going to get away from Carnarvon before sunset. I've just seen an old man coming down the street on a Chopper – a green Chopper from the seventies!

Once upon a time just about every boy in the country wanted a Chopper. Choppers had a small front wheel, three gears, tall handlebars, and a spiffy padded seat with a backrest. I run after the old man. He brakes and gets off. Jakob Jonkers is his name, he's sixty-six years old and this green Chopper is the only transport he's ever owned.

"Let me tell you, now: I got this bike in 1974. My father bought it for me from the Jacobs brothers' shop right there." He points down the road. "I keep fixing it up to keep it going. I can't ride any other kind of bicycle. I can't manage with them. They hurt my bum." He rubs the saddle with its linoleum patch. "This one's nice and soft. But it's not so easy to get parts any more. I struggle with tyres and tubes."

That's why he takes a car pump everywhere he goes, wrapped in a nose bag. One of the Chopper's other attractions was that you didn't pump the tyres with a bicycle pump. You had to go to the garage and use the pneumatic pump, like a car.

Oom Jakob jiggles the gear lever. "At least two of the gears still work, in a way." He taps the light with his finger. "There's nothing wrong with the light."

When it's a very dark night, he lowers the rectangular dynamo attached to the steering rod until it touches the front wheel. Then, as the dynamo sings, the light makes a tunnel through the darkness in front of the Chopper.

"I've ridden through pitch darkness on it. When it's pitch, pitch dark."

12.

Vosburg, on the other side of Carnarvon, must surely be the only town in the world that advertises its trees' shade. *Come and relax in the lovely shade of our trees,* reads the board at the entrance to the town.

In summer you'd be forgiven for thinking there's nothing but a screen door separating Carnarvon from hell, or at least that's how some locals describe the heat. Even during the great flood, others will tell you, they saw the lightning on the horizon towards Britstown, but there wasn't a drop of rain. This is a dry, beaten piece of land.

It's eleven o'clock on a perfectly ordinary Tuesday morning and there's no sign of life along Vosburg's main street. There are no shady trees either. I try calling Pa. We haven't talked since the angry conversation we had when I was in Van Wyksvlei. Since then, I haven't been able to put him out of my mind. Perhaps this is the first time I've really understood why we use the word fatherland. The father is the land, the land is the father. You can't deal with the one without dealing with the other.

I dial Pa's number. After a while a voice answers. "Hello. This is Ouboet's phone." It's Johannes Bogotsi. How and why this came about, I don't know, but he no longer addresses Pa as Oubaas and has been calling him Ouboet for the last few months. Sometimes they have coffee together at the table, each with his enamel mug.

"Can I speak to Ouboet, Johannes?" I ask.

It sounds as if Johannes has placed his hand over the phone because the voices at the other end are muffled. Then Johannes comes back: "Ouboet says he'll phone you back."

"Is he all right?" I ask.

Another muffled silence. Then Johannes says: "Ouboet says he's all right. He'll phone you."

"Is Ouboet angry with me?"

Johannes goes quiet again, then the connection is cut.

On a corner near the Vosburg post office I see a guy sitting on the curb. I drive slowly past him. He's dressed in the unofficial uniform of the Karoo: a colourful Pep shirt, blue Johnstone overall trousers, and velskoene. He has a packet of Boxer tobacco on his thigh and is busy rolling a zol. He slowly slides the edge of the paper to and fro between his lips, reaches for the matches in his breast pocket, and then I've passed him and can't see him any more.

A little further along, a signpost announces: *AE Motor Mac*. It's the head office of Awie Smit, the local motor mechanic. It's surrounded by a number of sad cars awaiting Awie's attention: a Datsun 1500, the front half of a Chev Fleetline bakkie, a Corolla with one yellow and one red front mudguard.

Oom Awie is standing behind the workshop next to a Nissan bakkie, contemplating the engine as if it's the sickbed of a loved one.

If you're not from here, it's easy to dismiss oom Awie with one glance and turn up your nose: oh, one of those. Just look at the dirty overall! The stump of a finger on his left hand! But wait till your car breaks down on the rough dirt road between here and Carnarvon with its second flat tyre or a hole in the radiator, and you'll be quick to ask for Awie's telephone number.

Oom Awie's in the mood for a chat. He sits on an upturned paint tin. The Nissan can wait. Besides, he's already been waiting for two days for the spares that are coming from Kimberley by courier.

"Have a seat." He gestures towards the paint tin next to him.

I sit down. It's beginning to feel as if my journey is veering off track. It feels more like a long farewell to the platteland as it once was.

Oupa, Pa's dad, was a mechanic in Memel in the Free State.

A mechanic in a small town has to be a man with a plan because spare parts are hard to come by. "I don't know whether it's true, but they say that some guys in the Kalahari used a driedoring stick to replace their plug wires." He gives a little laugh. "Apparently it works like a bomb when it's full of water. Water conducts electricity, you know. And when your bearings' liner packs in, you use a velskoen's sole. The sole soon wears so smooth that it looks like metal. Someone also told me once that they used to use ostrich fat for engine oil during the war."

Awie looks at the yard: the Datsun, the Fleetline, the Corolla. "I wish I could write down everything I know." He gives me an almost pleading look. "Why don't you write the story of my life? I can tell you lots of things. I can give you other guys' phone numbers. Smittie Smit from Hanover. He's a driller. He's been drilling for water in the Karoo for donkey's years. And talk to Emgee Swart at the exchange in Richmond. They still have a manual exchange." A silence. "Someone has to write about us. If no one does it, everyone will think our generation and those before us were all bad. We helped build this country."

I look at oom Awie sitting on the paint tin. Maybe I should write your story down, I think. Yours, and that of all the people and the old cars and drilling machines next to the road, without trying to understand. Maybe that's all this journey can be for me. Maybe that's all that remains for us to do in this country: to write everything down.

Oom Awie gets up and goes to the workshop to get Smittie Smit's phone number for me. I follow him. Hammers and screwdrivers and spanners hang from hooks on the wall, the outline of each marked with koki pen. He goes to search through his desk behind the glass partition in one corner. This workshop should be written about together with oom Awie: the hammers and the screwdrivers and the spanners against the wall, the STP sticker on the cupboard, the desk . . . Oh, there's much to write about on oom Awie's desk: a pocket calculator, a book with a red spine and curled pages filled with telephone numbers, an empty Peter Stuyvesant packet, an overflowing ashtray made from a car's piston. A stack of invoices on a metal skewer attached to a piece of wood. A Sanlam calendar.

"How many people live in Vosburg?" I ask as oom Awie walks me back to my bakkie. He answers without hesitation: "In the main town there are eighty-seven houses, forty-five are empty and thirteen for sale. The last time I counted, there were seventy-eight people living here."

He strokes his beard and starts listing the seventy-eight souls, like a litany. "Down there is Francois Conradie and his wife, Kobie. Then there's Louis de Lange, then the Hugos, then Koos Olivier and his family. Then there's Rolly Drake's house. He's dead now. Then it's the Barends' house, then the hospital, then Peter Griffith. Then you get to Bart and next to him are the De Klerks – the daughters and the mother. Then it's the co-op, then Eddie Oberholzer and his family. In that other street lives oom Willie Coetzee, then the bakery, then my brother-in-law. Then there's Kitty van Heerden. Old tannie Annie used to live next to her but now she's living with her daughter-in-law. Then there's Zelda from the garage, then the Van der Molens and then a house that's standing empty. Then it's Willem Bezuidenhout and next to him, Johan van Rensburg . . ."

13.

Why do these decrepit old rattletraps keep turning up wherever I go?

The other morning, about thirty kilometres from Britstown, a 1980s Datsun 1400 had broken down on the side of the road. On the back of it is a load of firewood and standing next to it, two guys. One waves an empty two-litre Coke bottle at me like a white flag as I approach.

I notice that the bakkie is white but the tailgate is yellow. The left back wheel is angled slightly towards the left. The exhaust pipe is held up by a piece of wire, and an orange mesh bag is tied to the grille. Reluctantly, I pull over.

One of the men hurries over. Colourful Pep Stores shirt. Blue Johnstone overall trousers. Velskoene. "I just need a lift to Brits-town, my larnie. We need petrol."

We, not the bakkie. Then I spot his friend in the rear-view mirror and he does look as if he's running on empty: he's leaning against the equally buggered bakkie, one elbow on the bonnet.

When I see someone standing next to the road with a bottle or a can, I often wonder how on earth it's possible to run out of petrol in that spot, where everything is so far away. Surely you check you have enough in your tank before setting off? Easy. Simple.

I reach over and open the bakkie door for him. He slides onto the seat next to me and brings with him the smell of wood and veld. His name is Fielies Syster.

As I'm about to drive off, the other guy knocks on the window on Fielies' side. Fielies opens it, and without a word, he takes a half-smoked cigarette and a box of matches out of his trouser pocket and hands them over. Is this something they agreed on beforehand? That the one who has to stay with the bakkie gets to finish the cigarette?

Fielies Syster is an unemployed fencer, sheep shearer and farm labourer. Now he and his friend collect wood in the veld and sell it to people in Britstown. On a good day, he can get R250 for a bakkie-load.

He's holding the Coke bottle between his knees and I notice some Coke sloshing around in the bottom. So he didn't plan to run out of petrol. It just happened. But how? Did he say to himself, okay, I don't have enough petrol but I'm going to hope for the best?

"It's my brother-in-law's fault, my larnie. He lied to me. He used the bakkie yesterday to fetch a bed in Victoria West for his ouma. When he brought it back this morning, he said he'd filled the tank again. So us two went to collect the wood and now we're stuck, because my brother-in-law lied. He didn't fill it up again."

"Didn't you check the petrol gauge?"

"But that hasn't worked in ages, my larnie."

14.

Pa still hasn't called. I said some harsh things to him when we last spoke, when I was in Van Wyksvlei. I didn't stop at the Broederbond. I also told him how awful it was during the almost eight years he was chaplain-general of the Afrikaner Weerstandsbeweging (AWB). He often appeared at parades, dressed in a khaki uniform and a maroon beret, with Eugène Terre'Blanche. He was the spiritual leader of people who wanted to force the country back into darkness.

At the filling station in Britstown, while the attendant fills the bakkie with diesel, I dial Pa's number again. It rings six times and then Johannes Bogotsi answers. "Hello. This is Ouboet's phone." The same as last time.

"Where's Ouboet?" I ask. "What are you doing?"

"I'm sitting with Ouboet in his room. I rubbed his feet with some medicine." Because of Pa's weak heart, his feet often become swollen when his body retains too much water.

"Can I talk to Ouboet?" I ask.

Silence – the same muffled silence as before. Then Johannes's voice: "Ouboet says he'll phone you."

"Tell Ouboet I'm going to Daniëlskuil."

"Daniëlskuil," says Johannes. And again, "Daniëlskuil."

"Tell Ouboet that's where I'm going."

Pa was the dominee there for many years, and I know he'd like to go back there again. Perhaps he'll call to ask me about it.

15.

Emgee Swart leans towards the switchboard of the manual exchange behind the Richmond post office. One of the farmers in the area has called. "It's André Kok." Emgee points to the light and the small vibrating switch on the switchboard. "That's André's ring. His wife Elmarie has a different one."

Emgee pushes a button. "Telkom, Richmond. Good evening," he says. "Well, thank you. And you? Ja. Ja . . . Let me ring them. Hold on a second . . ."

After twenty years at the town's telephone exchange, Emgee recognises people by the way they turn the handle at the other end. He pushes another few buttons. "Going through," he says and plugs the connecting cord into a hole. "You can talk now."

It's just after nine o'clock in the evening, and Emgee is working night shift. I arrived from Britstown this afternoon, had a bite at the Vet Muis Plaaskombuis, and now I'm here with Emgee. I feel as if I've been transported back to the seventies, when every dorp in the country still had a manual telephone exchange.

"In this job, you develop a very good memory." Emgee doesn't take his eyes off the buttons and lights before him. "You have to remember names, you have to remember numbers, you have to remember everything."

I hear a dog barking somewhere in the dark outside and the sigh of a truck as it engages a lower gear on the N1. It's sixty kilometres to Hanover, the next dorp.

I've never been in this room before, yet everything in it is vaguely familiar: the switchboard, the steel cabinet in the corner, the bed against the wall, the rubber plant in the brown plastic pot, the picture of the three monkeys against the wall: *See no evil, Hear no evil, Speak no evil.*

All of us who have ties with the platteland have an exchange like this somewhere in our past – an old manual exchange.

The one in Daniëlskuil where I grew up wasn't much different. Tannie Julia Virtue sat where Emgee is sitting now, wearing a set of headphones.

In 1970, forty-one years ago, there were almost a thousand exchanges like this in the country – in large towns like Paarl and Kimberley and Pietersburg, but also in small settlements like Bitterfontein and Beestekraal and Babanango. Kliprivier. Kameel. Koekenaap.

"In the old days we were eight on a shift," says Emgee. "All you could see were lights flashing all over the board."

That was when there were four hundred homes and businesses with crank telephones in the town and surrounding area. Now there are nineteen party lines shared by seventy-eight farmers and serviced by Emgee and the rest of the exchange team.

In the entire country there are just thirty-three manual telephone exchanges left, all of them servicing party lines.

No one in South Africa has more experience of working a manual exchange than Emgee. Two weeks ago he got his certificate for forty years' service. Not counting Richmond, he's been to seventy-seven exchanges, either to work there, as a substitute, or to train operators.

He's even been to Kamieskroon deep in Namaqualand to train someone called Faans on the switchboard. "The people in that part of the world struggle to speak English, you know. But Faans did well. Eventually I left him to carry on by himself while I went walking around town. One evening I decided to phone from the phone booth to test him. 'Good evening, sir,' I said. 'I want to make a call.' I could hear Faans going quiet. The next minute he came running out of the exchange, shouting: 'Emgee! Emgee! Help! English! English!'"

A green light flashes on the switchboard. It's someone from outside Richmond who'd like to talk to one of the local farmers. Again

Emgee answers: "Telkom, Richmond. Good evening . . . double one one two? Let me try them."

Each farmer has his own ring. The last two digits of the number determine the ring. The ring for 1112 is a short ring followed by two long ones. For 1121 it's two short rings followed by a long one.

Without an experienced operator like Emgee, a party line could be a recipe for animosity and arguments. Because there's only one line for up to ten farmers, only one can make or receive a call at a time. That's why Emgee times each call. After three minutes he interrupts and tells the people on the line: "Three minutes are up." That way, no one can lose track of time.

And because people share the same line, they can also eavesdrop. Problems, problems, problems.

Everyone who's ever encountered a manual exchange has an eavesdropping story. Like the one about the woman who got so carried away by two farmers' conversation about politics that she chipped in: "Now you're lying, you bloody Saps!"

Emgee looks at the switchboard. Another call.

It's almost like watching the last remnants of an old, old ritual being repeated every time Emgee answers: "Telkom, Richmond. Good evening . . . Ja. Ja . . . The clouds are looking promising. We may get rain . . . Ja . . . Soon, I think . . . Okay, I'm ringing them . . ."

An old ritual that speaks of the importance of human contact.

He often gets calls from pigeon fanciers: "What's the weather like over there, Emgee? Is it windy?" He regularly has to give directions, too, and has even helped children with their homework.

While working in Laingsburg one evening, he had to help a man call Princess Diana. "This guy had a thing for Princess Di," Emgee remembers. "One evening, after he'd had a glass or two of wine, he called and asked us to put him through to England, to Princess Di. We can't refuse to transfer a call, it's the law. So I asked our international exchange in Cape Town to connect me with Buckingham Palace."

It wasn't easy, but eventually the call went through to the palace. Then, in his best Laingsburg English, the man asked: "Can I speak to Lady Di, please?" It took him a while to realise he was talking to an answering machine. It was late, and the palace was closed.

And then there's the time Emgee was on duty here in Richmond with Bertie Theron, another operator. A call came in quite late that evening. Bertie answered and it was a woman from Italy. It's not impossible to get a crossed line or connection, so a call from the other side of the world does sometimes come through here. Bertie was very excited. An Italian from Italy? Here in the Karoo? "Italy, you say?" he shouted excitedly. "You genuine from Italy? Italy, like in overseas? It's wonderful! It's beautiful! To prove this that you're really from Italy, can you please send me a postcard, please . . ."

Bertie gave her his address and, can you believe it, a week or three later a postcard arrived in Richmond from Italy, addressed to "Berpie Tron".

Bertie's dead now. Oom Schalk Pieterse, who also worked here for donkey's years, is dead too. He's the one who went to the hospital to beg for the bed against the wall and brought it back here. If you're on night duty, you're allowed to sleep on duty.

Between the buttons and levers I see the faint paths that Emgee and other operators' fingers have traced on the switchboard over the years. Lists with telephone numbers are stuck up everywhere. Over there is a calendar with a photograph of the sun setting over the ocean.

Every exchange, no matter how small, also has an official evacuation plan somewhere on a wall in case fire should break out.

Emgee points to a row of small holes in the switchboard that look like dark eyes. There's a red metal plate around them. These were the connections for the coin-operated phones in town – the tickey-boxes at the hotel and the school hostel and the garage and a few other places.

A tickey-box was often a source of great aggravation for switchboard operators. Chances were that the person on the other end was in trouble: stranded hitchhikers, late-night drunks, frightened soldiers or homesick children, guys whose girlfriends had broken up with them and women who'd had to flee their husbands' fists.

"Sometimes people cheated and used a langtiekie," Emgee says. "It wasn't easy to catch them. And it was popular, especially with the schoolchildren from the hostel. They'd attach a five-cent coin to a piece of sellotape and slide it down the tickey-box's slot. As soon as it went past the sensor, it made a prrr sound, as if the coin had dropped into the money box. But they'd pull it back up and use the same coin again and again . . ."

Later, the design of coin-operated phones was changed to stop people from doing this.

This was also the time of the collect call, something that was quite complicated.

"Hello, please may I make a collect call to my parents, Oom," I hear my own pleading voice from a tickey-box at De Aar station or some such desperate place.

First you had to ask the operator whether you could do it. Then he would say: "Okay. What's the number?" You gave him the number. Then he'd call the switchboard operator in your town. The operator would ring your parents' number and ask: "Sir, are you willing to accept a collect call from your son?" Luckily, Pa usually agreed to pay for the call. Then the operator you had first spoken to came back and said: "Okay, going through . . ."

The more I think of manual exchanges, the more voices I hear coming back to me. Daniëlkuil's tant Julia saying: "Number, please." Or: "No, wait, your parents aren't at home. I think they went to visit tant Hester. Let me try there . . ."

Or my late mother lifting the handset and asking: "Busy?"

Or old Souf, the Griqua tannie who worked for us in Daniëlskuil and who always, irrespective of who might be calling, had the same refrain: "Hello, Miss. You can talk, please."

Emgee goes to the back of the switchboard. The lines have become quiet. "Come look here." He points to the top of the switchboard and there it is: an old Siemens crank telephone. The real McCoy. Pitch black. And I can hear tannie Julia saying: "Hold on for a trunk call."

There was a time when hundreds and thousands of homes had one of these.

This one still works. Emgee pushes a button on the switchboard and the familiar, long-forgotten trill echoes through the room. It's a cross between a bicycle bell and a triangle in a school percussion band.

The telephone used to have a place of honour in the home. Older models were attached to a wall in the passage or the dining-room. In more modern homes they often sat on a cane table in the passage. A stack of telephone directories was always within reach, as well as an address book with an alphabetical index crammed with numbers.

The spot on the wall above the telephone was reserved for the church calendar, where birthdays, weddings and important rugby matches were marked.

Emgee can't say how much longer it will be before there are no manual exchanges left in South Africa. Perhaps there will be fewer than thirty-three by this time next year. Who knows? Party lines are expensive to maintain, and besides, there are few places in the country that don't have cellphone reception.

On the ridge outside town, the whitewashed stones no longer spell RICHMOND. The town got its own website, and just the other day people went up there to place more stones on the ridge. It now says WWW.RICHMOND.CO.ZA.

Emgee returns to his chair at the switchboard. Outside, the dog is still barking as another truck rumbles past. On the switchboard, a light starts flashing like an SOS from a world that is long gone.

16.

It's close to midnight. I've booked into the overnight rooms behind the Caltex garage in Richmond, but I can't sleep. I'd left my cellphone in the bakkie while visiting Emgee Swart at the exchange. When I got back, there were four missed calls from Pa but no message. I feel as if I'm on the road to nowhere. My trip is bogged down in nostalgia. I suck the peppermint that's been waiting on my bed and page through my notebook, looking for the page with my notes on nostalgia. It also contains my notes on the Snyman family. *Ancestor*, it says at the top. *Christoffel Snyman, son of Hans Christoffel Schneider and Groot Catrijn.* I'll have to talk to Pa about that. Or should I spare him this detail? Then I find what I'm looking for: nostalgia. The word stems from the Greek *nostos* (return) and *algos* (suffering). The word nostalgia – or *nostalgos* – was first used in 1688 by German doctor Johannes Hofer to describe a mental condition he initially observed among soldiers who were homesick while fighting in a foreign country. As his study of nostalgia progressed, Hofer noticed that it's not just soldiers in foreign countries who suffer from nostalgia. Anyone who feels he's lost his fatherland can experience it. Among the symptoms Hofer identified were an abiding sadness and feeling of bereavement, persistent thoughts of the fatherland, disturbed sleep patterns, palpitations, disturbed thoughts and a stubborn obsession with the fatherland. Hofer also notes that it's not only people who are homesick for their fatherland who experience nostalgia; the condition can even be found in someone whose fatherland has changed and become unfamiliar to him.

17.

The trucks come and go in a never-ending stream at the truck-stop next to the N1 at Hanover. Some drivers get out, stretch their legs, perhaps buy something at the café, and disappear into the night again: to Cape Town, to Gauteng, even across the border, north, into Africa.

Others sleep here, in the cabs of their trucks.

It's six o'clock in the morning and I haven't slept much. I have an appointment to meet Smittie Smit in town a little later. He's one of the master borehole drillers of the Karoo. But for now I'm sitting in the café at the truck stop and reading the *Graaff-Reinet Advertiser* and listening to the truck drivers who come in and order food and coffee from the man behind the counter.

"Can I have two toasted cheese 'n chips. With lots of Worcester sauce on the chips."

"Two toasted cheese?"

"Yes. Or rather no. Make it three."

"Three toasted cheese."

"Yes, three."

"With chips?"

"Yes. With chips. And I want plenty Worcester sauce."

"Do you want chips with all three?"

"Yes! Fuck! I told you. With lots of Worcester sauce."

"What's wrong with you this morning?"

"I'm pissed off with my boss. How are things with you?"

My phone rings on the table next to the newspaper. It's Pa. He sounds woozy. "Your pa's struggling to sleep, son. I tried calling you last night." He's slurring his words. He hasn't put his false teeth in yet. His thinning hair is sticking up wildly. I can picture him. I know what he looks like in the mornings.

"Are you in Daniëlskuil yet, son? Johannes says that's where you're going."

"I'm still on my way, Pa."

"Be careful. I'm going to try and get some sleep again. I'm struggling to breathe. I just wanted to check you're safe."

I want to apologise for my harsh words but he's already gone.

Maybe this is how the love between a father and son works, because it's how it's always been with us: we'd argue, Pa and I, then one would make a conciliatory move, and then we'd pretend nothing had happened. Until the next time, when the same old things often got rehashed.

There's an article in the *Graaff-Reinet Advertiser* about pigeon fanciers in the area whose racing pigeons got mixed up with birds belonging to pigeon fanciers from the Cape.

VICTORIA WEST. – The weekend's race from Laingsburg was an absolute disaster. Without a doubt, the reason for this was the large flocks of pigeons that flew to Cape Town and the small number of our pigeons that flew home.

Thirty thousand pigeons were released from Beaufort West on Saturday and 12 000 from Victoria West. It is not surprising that our pigeons had such a difficult time. We've already heard that one of Louis and Maritza's pigeons is with someone in Kraaifontein.

By Saturday evening many pigeons throughout the union have not yet returned. It was worrying for everyone because we are attached to each and every one of our pigeons.

I read and reread the article three or five times, as if it has to have a deeper meaning, and the restaurant door behind me opens with a whistle and then slams shut. A new voice addresses the young chap behind the counter: "Two double cheeseburgers, please."

"With chips?"

"Yes, why not? A man gets hungry."

"Have you been driving all night?"

"I slept for an hour or so just now, until that woman woke me up with her screams."

"What woman?"

"I didn't see her. Screamed like a mad thing. I don't know if someone was beating her up or what."

Overnight truck-stops like this have cropped up in many towns. Always somewhere on the outskirts. Sometimes when I'm in a strange dorp and can't sleep, I go to the truck-stop. The café never closes and there are always voices to listen to.

It's at this truck-stop that I first met Kitte – Kitte Honiball, an old drifter who does odd jobs every now and then before hitting the road again. When I met him he'd been on his way to Port Elizabeth with a windsurfer and a dog called Boetie, but these days he's in Vanderbijlpark. Sometimes he sends me a please-call-me.

In the open space in front of the café there are around ten or fifteen trucks. I see two cigarettes glowing in the dark inside one of them. Elsewhere, someone is listening to boeremusiek on the radio. Someone else keeps blowing his nose: blow, blow, blow.

It strikes me that many truck owners like to call their companies after themselves: PA Verhoef Transport, Slabbert Burger, Kobus Hartzer, Steynberg.

Each truck is supposed to have a satellite tracking system, so each driver's movements can be traced in detail on a computer in an office in Johannesburg or Durban or wherever.

Towards the east, the sky behind the ridges starts turning silver and then red. Two doves are sitting on the telephone line across the road. A girl enters the café. I watch her. She's wearing a skimpy black skirt and black shoes with thin, high heels. Just behind her ankles, a strip of plaster is sticking out above her shoes, maybe to stop them from chafing. She buys a packet of Beechies, two Panados and a can of Coke Light. Then she leaves, click-clack on her heels, as a truck turns in at the gate. For a second she looks as if she's going to start running, but she doesn't. Outside the gate she bends down and takes off the high heels and walks down the street, carrying them in her hand.

The night is over, for now.

18.

Divining water isn't as simple as cutting a forked stick from a tree. This I realise the minute Smittie Smit goes to work in the veld just outside Hanover in the Karoo. It's a serious business.

For a start, it needs to be the right sort of forked stick. "Bloubos works well," he says. "But I prefer one of these." He holds up the stick he's brought with him. "Driedoring bush."

He grips the two legs of the fork in his large hands and pulls them apart so that the third leg points to the sky like an arrow. Then, slowly, he takes a step, then another, and another. As if by itself, the stick starts turning in Smittie's hands . . .

"There's a dolerite seam under here," he says as he stops. "If you drill on either side of it, you'll find water."

Smittie may not have a university degree in geology, but walking with him in the veld near his house, I get the impression he can just about see into the earth. He points out the dolerite seam, chats about the various dolerite rock formations and the dolomite. In between, he lets me in on a few secrets: wherever you see reeds growing in the veld, you know the water table is shallow. A clump of bloubos growing in a more or less straight line is a good indicator of underground water too.

At sixty-three, Smittie is a legend in the Karoo and Northern Cape. Just ask the farmers around Victoria West and Vosburg, at Britstown, even as far as Vryburg. Many will say you won't find a better water diviner or a more reliable driller than Smittie Smit.

He's been travelling all over for almost forty-six years with his drill, his forked stick and his caravan. Most of the time his wife,

Hantie, accompanies him in the veld. At the moment, they're taking a break and have come to spend a few days at their home in Hanover, but they'll be back on the road soon, to Carnarvon almost four hundred kilometres away. To see a farmer whose boreholes are drying up.

"Whenever people's water run out," says Smittie, "we try and help."

He drops his forked stick and we turn back to the house. He just wanted to show me more or less how he works. His house at the bottom end of Rawstone Street is some distance away from the others. It reminds me of oom Bennie Vermeulen: he was the driller in Daniëlskuil and his house also stood apart from the others, on the edge of town.

For many people in the area, oom Bennie brought as much hope as Pa, who was a church minister. Yet oom Bennie didn't have the same status as Pa.

In oom Bennie's yard there were several broken pieces of machinery and cars, and there were always a few geese waddling about. When oom Bennie wasn't drilling somewhere in the district, his drill stood under the pepper tree – it was a scuffed red thing with fat tyres that he towed with a Thames lorry.

Smittie's yard is a lot tidier. He keeps his drilling paraphernalia at a workshop in the dorp. We go through to the sitting room and tannie Hantie brings a tray with coffee and biscuits. In the corner, on the carpet, is a scale model of a drill Smittie made for Leon Wilkenson, one of his grandsons. The boy is twelve and has a healthy interest in drilling.

"To be honest, I'm afraid everything I know will be lost one day," says Smittie. "I want to pass it on to someone, because the drilling business is changing a lot. The things I know aren't written in text books. You can't learn it at university." He taps his head. "It's in here."

Nowadays, a lot of drilling is done by companies that own a fleet of drilling machines – pneumatic drills fitted onto the back of trucks. Some drillers even call themselves "drill machine technicians" and work with a geologist or someone using geological equipment designed to find water.

Drillers and water diviners like Smittie are a dying breed: men with big forearms and rough hands and weather-beaten faces full of lines and wrinkles. Or perhaps I should say "summer-beaten" because it's the summers that ravage their faces.

Smittie's father, also called Smittie, was a driller too. He bought a jumper drill in 1962, a red one just like oom Bennie Vermeulen's. In those days, just about every jumper drill in the country was red and made by Dreyer Engineering Works in Bloemfontein.

Smittie started out as a driller with his dad, using that old Dreyer, towed by a Chev lorry.

"In the early years we didn't have a caravan. We slept in the Chev, my pa on the seat and me on the floor. In the evenings we braaied."

At first he didn't divine water himself. "Water divining is a funny business. Sometimes you find a hole for someone, oh . . . but then you don't find decent water. That's the worst, to drive away from a customer when you haven't been successful.

"There are farmers who will tell you straight: 'Don't come near my farm with a stick. Do you hear?' It's everyone's right to say that. Others say divining water with a stick is the devil's work." Smittie shakes his head. How can it be the devil's work if he's a Christian and a man of the church?

Yet other farmers – and these days there are a lot of them – call in a geologist to find a borehole for them.

Again Smittie shakes his head. A geologist? Hmph. It's not that he doesn't trust a geologist's expertise. On the contrary. On the table in front of us is a geology encyclopaedia. It's just that what the handbook says doesn't always work in practice. He's seen it many times.

"Tell him about that hole outside Britstown," tannie Hantie, who has joined us by now, eggs him on.

It was a few years ago when the tarred road between Britstown and Victoria West was being built. The roadworkers urgently needed water to finish the road, but after they'd tried twenty or so bore-holes they still didn't have enough. It was a crisis.

By then Smittie had replaced the Dreyer with a pneumatic drill. As most drillers had. The Dreyer's lethargic pounding had become too slow for the demands of the modern world. With a Dreyer you could barely manage to drill two metres into dolomite, and only on a good day, whereas a pneumatic drill lets you do fifty metres over the same period.

The roadworkers phoned him. Come and help us, Smittie. We don't know which way to turn. "I could hear they were desperate," says Smittie. "I was still working on a hole at Middelburg, but I finished up there, hooked up my rig and drove to Britstown. 'How can I help you, boys?' I asked. 'We're looking for water, Smittie. We must finish this road,' they said. 'Where do you want me to drill?' I asked. 'You decide,' they said. Now, you must know that these were professors and groundwater experts who'd found those twen-ty useless holes." He shakes his head again. Groundwater experts. Hmph.

He told the roadworkers to leave him alone and took out his forked stick to try it out here and there. "Some days when I'm walk-ing with my stick something just tells me this is the day I'm going to find a lot of water." He's quiet for a second. "I think it's my faith that helps me."

The spot to drill, he decided, was on a dolerite bank on the farm Wolwekraal, right next to the road that was waiting to be built. The road builders got permission from the farmer, Pieter Jooste, and Smittie set up his pneumatic drill.

"Many people laughed and said he was crazy," says tannie Hantie.

Smittie gives a wry laugh. The people also laughed at Noah when he built the ark. Smittie switched on the drill, and then it was just him against that dolerite. It took two days to break through, while the group of people who came to mock kept growing.

"You must know, I was sitting at the caravan," says tannie Hantie. "I saw everything. More and more farmers came, and it was hot,

94

and they came to sit in the shade of the caravan and carried on bad-mouthing my husband. Some people think they're better than others. They watched him and said things like: 'These drillers are really sly. They know they aren't going to find water but they drill anyway and the road people have to pay.'"

On the third day, Smittie hit a stream underneath the dolerite seam. The water streamed from the hole: 135 000 litres an hour.

"I don't take pleasure in it. I just believe in what I do."

These days Smittie charges R220 for every metre he drills, but sometimes, well . . . "I get to a farmer and he says: 'Man, I only have money for fifty metres.' Then you get to fifty metres without finding water, but everything looks promising. What can you do? Then you drill deeper. That same guy will pay you back when he has a good year."

The deepest hole he's drilled was a hundred and fifty metres. But that's not the hole in the story people around here like to tell. That hole, the story goes, was so deep that the weight of the pipes running down it pulled the windmill into the hole. Eventually only the tail was visible above the ground.

"Tell him about that ninety-year-old oom in Carnarvon, Smittie," tannie Hantie coaxes again.

That would have been old oom Muller. Smittie drilled a borehole on his farm. For days the old Dreyer churned the insides of the earth, and then the water came.

"Oom Muller started to cry," says Smittie. "Then he asked us to help him to take off his shoes. So we helped him and he walked around in the water that came out of the hole, barefoot and crying."

Of course there have also been angry, disappointed farmers on farms where he couldn't find water. He can't deny it. That's how it is. That's life.

Again Smittie is quiet. He can't say how much longer he'll be able to carry on. He's not getting any younger. Young Leon, his grandson, often goes with him, and then Smittie tells him everything he knows. Maybe, just maybe, the boy will become a driller one day.

"He's keen. I can only hope. Do you know that all the drillers I know are between sixty and seventy years old? We all know one another." One by one he counts them off. "There's oom Jan du Plessis in Beaufort West. Oom Jan van Zyl in Prieska. Ockert Oosthuizen is between Colesberg and Venterstad. Graaff-Reinet has the Retiefs . . ."

Smittie doesn't know what became of his old Dreyer; he sold it long ago. Maybe someone broke it up and sold it for scrap metal.

He knows of only one Dreyer in the area and that belongs to Doy Ferreira, a driller from Philipstown about sixty kilometres away. Oom Doy apparently uses it to clean out overgrown boreholes for farmers.

I have to see a Dreyer one more time, I decide, and head for Philipstown, but oom Doy isn't home. His Dreyer isn't around either. At the Ebenhaeser Garage, which he owns, there are five or six broken Lister engines. Seeing them makes me wonder how many boreholes in South Africa have Lister engines standing right next to them, puff-puff-puffing water into a tank or a dam or a trough.

Marnie van Wyk tells me about Johan Louw, who may still have a Dreyer. The only problem is that Johan is in Philippolis, about a hundred and forty kilometres from Philipstown.

Later that afternoon, I drive into Philippolis under low clouds. It's just been raining. The radio in the bakkie is tuned to RSG and Amore Bekker's talk show is on. She's talking to someone called Thinus about his chicken recipe:

> AMORE: I believe you call it your fruity chicken, Thinus. Tell us how you make it.
> THINUS: You see, Amore, you add your spices, Aromat and so on. Then you take the chicken and boil it until you can take all the bones out.
> AMORE: And then?
> THINUS: Then you take out all the bones and throw the chicken in another pot.
> AMORE: And then?

THINUS: Then you throw four bananas and four apples in the pot with the empty chicken.

AMORE: That sounds interesting.

THINUS: Yes, ja, Amore. You can throw in any fruit you feel like. I won't recommend papaya but a pineapple works too.

AMORE: And then?

THINUS: Then you add 125 millilitres of chutney and curry, as much as you want. Then you boil everything for about half an hour.

AMORE: And then it's ready?

THINUS: Then it's ready to eat, Amore.

Johan Louw is sitting in The Workshop, a bar next to the only garage in Philippolis. He's wearing his blue overall trousers and a stetson-like hat on his head. It's not for nothing that the locals call him Die Grensvegter, after the pulp fiction hero.

He's been a driller for over thirty years. He also repairs windmills and confirms that he owns a Dreyer. "I'll show you, but can I finish my beer first?"

The afternoon light is gentle when we drive to Johan's small-holding outside town. We turn onto a narrow road. Then we come to a yard that reminds me a little of oom Bennie Vermeulen's. There's a Ferguson Vaaljapie tractor under a rusty lean-to; and then there it is, with its fat tyres and cables and levers. Red and scarred. *Manufactured by Dreyer Eng Works. PO Box 682, BFN, OFS.* The letters are painted on the shaft head which is closed.

Johan strokes the shaft with one rough hand. "This is a helluva thing. A helluva thing."

19.

While I was at Johan Louw's smallholding looking at his Dreyer, Pa called and left a message. But I decide to take Johan back to The Workshop first, and then drive out on the road to Fauresmith and Jagersfontein. From there the road leads to Koffiefontein and Jacobsdal. To Daniëlskuil.

Once I reach the outskirts of town, I pull over and return Pa's call.

He answers almost immediately, a sign that he's sitting at the kitchen table. He hasn't sounded this cheerful in days.

"What are you doing?" I ask. "Is everything all right there?"

"I'm making macaroni and cheese, son."

For years, Pa has made macaroni and cheese on special occasions. Maybe, because meat has always been the staple food in our home, he sees macaroni and cheese as exotic.

"I'm sitting here with the map in front of me, son," he says. "You know how far you have to drive to get to Daniëlskuil from where you are, don't you?"

Clearly Pa is with me in spirit on the road to Daniëlskuil.

"No," I lie. "How far do I have to go, Pa? I'm in Philippolis."

It's quiet at the other end. I can see him paging through his old Shell road map. Over the years, some of the pages have come loose.

"Are you still there?" he asks after a while. "The best would be to drive from Philippolis to Jagersfontein and Fauresmith, and from there to Koffiefontein and Jacobsdal."

"Thanks, Pa. That's a great help."

"I can't remember when last I was in Daniëlskuil, son. I wish I could go there again. I wonder how big the trees that I planted have grown. Can Pa ask you something else?"

"Of course, Pa. Ask."

"Do you remember last year when we went to Memel?"

"Of course I remember."

"It would be nice to go on a trip like that again. The two of us. But this time we'll go to Blood River and Pietermaritzburg, to the Church of the Covenant. I also want to go and see oupa Coenraad's trousers in the museum."

"Oupa's trousers? In the museum? Where did you hear that, Pa?"

"From Nooi." Nooi is Pa's stepsister.

"But why are they keeping the trousers there, Pa?"

"Oupa Coenraad was a very big man, son. They called him the Strongman of the Great Trek."

I expect nothing will have changed in Daniëlskuil and nothing will have remained the same either. The Dutch Reformed Church, a facebrick building from the sixties, with its slate roof, will still be there next to the parsonage – a facebrick building from the seventies, with a slate roof, where we used to live. Will the clock in the steeple still work? Maybe. Maybe not. In many dorps the clock in the church's steeple has stopped.

Maybe the paint is peeling from the town hall in the small square, and maybe the Commercial Hotel is now a lodge, with French furniture from Kimberley in the lounge and a Roman statue next to a pond in the courtyard. Oom Mike's café will still be on the corner, but I've heard somewhere that oom Mike has died. Maybe a Pakistani now sells cellphones and cheap televisions from oom Mike's café. Maybe tannie Julia from the exchange will still be there? And oom Bennie Vermeulen, the driller?

It always amazes me how quickly a dorp can change. I see it happening everywhere.

Not too long ago, the main streets of biggish towns all looked more or less the same: a church, a municipal office, a town hall and a library, a hotel, a branch office of one or two commercial banks, a general dealer that slowly turned into a grocery store, an Avbob funeral parlour, a home industry and a general outfitter.

Then one day the general dealer disappears. It becomes a Spar, an OK Foods or a Friendly Grocer. The bank's branch office closes – it's rationalisation, the manager explains – and alterations are done and it's divided into two smaller spaces: one for a China shop and the other for a cash loans business. The general outfitter becomes a Pep Stores and when next you decide to pop in at the home industry, you're faced with a row of fruit machines.

I drive through Jagersfontein and Fauresmith, further into the countryside. Everywhere, I come across the changing faces and rhythms of the dorps. The emphasis now, it seems, is on airtime, on cash loans, cheap clothes and cheap food and cheap furniture, Lotto and a decent funeral.

At the garage in Koffiefontein a young man presses a pamphlet into my hand as I wait for the petrol attendant to fill the diesel tank:

> Laphumikwezi Funeral Broker. In dignity we serve!
> Our Funeral Service Package
> Collection & preparation of deceased
> Graveside arrangements & decoration
> Carpeting for the family members area
> Coffin
> Hearse
> Coffin spray
> Hundred programs
> Big tent & catering
> Fifty chairs & four tables

Until his death, author Etienne Leroux farmed and wrote books on the farm Ja-Nee outside Koffiefontein. The Central Hotel, where Leroux apparently sometimes hung out, sitting erect on a bar stool in the corner with one elbow on the counter and his sunglasses and the legendary three packets of cigarettes he's said to have had with him at all times.

100

But the Central Hotel no longer exists.

The farm where he farmed for years is about ten kilometres out-side the dorp, on the Petrusville and Jacobsdal road. I stop there. There's an odd structure at the gate. It's built of concrete and stone. The farm's name is written on it in black letters: J N E. The gate is locked. It now belongs to a Schreuder, I gather, because there's another sign that reads: *Schreuder Boerdery.* The farmhouse stands among tall trees, with an empty swimming pool and neglected tennis court nearby.

This is where Etienne Leroux, the pen name of Stephen le Roux, wrote nearly all his books.

A man wearing brown overalls walks over from the direction of the farmhouse.

He was just a child in 1989 when Leroux died and was buried on a koppie on Wachenmakersdrift, the farm across the road, the farm that belonged to Leroux's father.

"He was good man, that one," says the man in the brown overalls. "He wasn't aggressive. My father first went to work for him. I was still small. One time, that man said to me: 'You have to speak Afri-kaans properly, man. You don't say *twak,* you say *tabak.'*"

Before I leave, I ask him for his name.

"My name is Stephen, Baas."

Some time ago, I copied a passage from one of Leroux's books into my notebook. It's from an essay he wrote about the Free State countryside: *To write about any place is to generalise. Who among us knows the whole truth? For generations, a small group of people will live in a certain area. Over time, they begin to develop certain behavioural and moral codes. Does that determine their nature? And, when the tarred roads are built and the communication net-works are developed, does that not also change the people and the landscape? It is happening all over the world, but here, where you have close bonds with the earth and the surroundings, the disas-ter that is transformation looks far bigger.*

20.

Not far from Jacobsdal, a tired old bakkie looms up in front of me. *Another* one.

At first it seems to be a Mazda, but when I get closer I see it's a Toyota, a pale blue 1970s Hilux with a mountain of stuff on the back: two hollow mattresses, a chair with golden tassels, a trunk with a dented lid, stuff like that. Old, used stuff.

Among all of this sits a man with a small brindle mongrel in his arms.

I always end up behind a bakkie like this, hopelessly overloaded and on its way somewhere with a dark cloud of smoke behind it.

I haven't heard the word in the Northern Cape, but in townships further north the people call an old car like this a "skorokoro". When we come to a slight bend in the road, I see that the driver of this particular skorokoro is one of those guys who leans to one side behind the wheel as he drives, with the window open and one arm clamped over the door.

I slow down and start to make a mental list of everything on the back: a wire cage with some chickens, a roll of chicken wire, a cooler box without a lid, a bunch of onions, a pair of gumboots.

At that moment, Martelize Brink is broadcasting birthday wishes on RSG: " . . . and in Montagu we have a young lady who is turning ninety-six today. Tannie Anna Immelman from Toevlucht Old-Age Home. Jonker and Letitia in Worcester would like to congratulate tannie on her birthday. We wish her God's richest blessings and may the year ahead be a wonderful one . . ."

It's as if gravity doesn't apply on the back of these bakkies:

things are stacked on top of more things, a milk urn on a battered suitcase on an old Telefunken TV set, until the stack towers above the cab. A bicycle, half a bag of flour, a three-legged cast-iron pot, two plastic tubs. The big, heavy things aren't necessarily packed at the bottom with the smaller things on top. Right at the top of this load, tied down with string, is a tattered couch and a table.

Who are these people? Where did they come from? Where are they going?

The bakkie skorokoros through the potholes in Jacobsdal's streets, past the Spar, through the outskirts of town, to the township.

It's the same story as everywhere else in the country: row upon row of shacks surround the brick houses. Everywhere you look, children are playing and men sit around, smoking and chatting. And everywhere, women are carrying buckets of water on their heads.

Suddenly, the Hilux slows down even more. It's getting ready to turn, that's clear. This kind of bakkie almost comes to a standstill before taking a corner, and when it does turn, it goes wide – wide and without indicating.

Is it because three or four people are squashed in next to the driver that he has to go so wide around a corner, because there isn't room for his arms to move freely?

The bakkie stops outside a small house with a yellow door. The driver gets out first, then the passenger door opens and a young man wearing a green cap with the South African flag on it appears. He's followed by a boy, a young girl, and a woman with a small child in her arms.

The driver notices me and comes over. "Can I help you, Baas?" he asks, and looks at me suspiciously.

His name is Edward Nacozama and it's his Hilux, but he's not the one who's moving. "It's them." He points to the man with the cap who got out on the passenger side of the bakkie. "He's my cousin. I'm just helping him."

I explain that I'm driving around the country and taking photographs and looking at things.

The man on the back clambers off the pile of stuff and puts the dog down.

"What's the dog's name?"

"Ogies, Baas."

Ogies lifts his leg and leaves a black line of pee on the bakkie's dusty back tyre.

It's not uncommon for township dogs to have Afrikaans names: Ogies, Vlekkie, Strepies, Witpoot.

The man with the cap – the one who is moving – comes over too. Daniël Morakile.

His wife, Jessica Top, comes to stand a little behind him, still holding the child. The child is wearing a pink jacket with Mickey Mouse on it.

Daniël is about to start explaining, but a woman with a colourful headscarf comes out of the house and calls them. In Tswana.

"It's her mother." Daniël points to Jessica. "We have to go and talk to her."

They approach the woman. They don't embrace and kiss; they talk. They're speaking Tswana and they sound despondent. After a while the woman goes back inside the house, still talking, with Daniël and the rest following her, still talking too.

"Eish, that guy has problems," says Edward. "They chased him away from the farm."

The prodigal son-in-law has found his way home at last.

Two bicycle tyres, three pots, a fishing rod, a flour tin.

Daniël was a labourer on a farm in the district for over five years, Edward tells me, but he and the farmer have been having problems lately. Now he has been fired and they're coming to ask if they can live here with Jessica's mother.

It's not clear why Daniël was fired. He says something about irrigation valves that someone else didn't close, but he got blamed for. In any case, it doesn't matter. He and his family need a roof over their heads by nightfall.

The Hilux's odometer has stopped at 89 763 kilometres. Edward's had it for seventeen years. He charges anything from R200 to help someone move, depending on the distance. It seems the volume of stuff isn't really a factor in determining the fee.

"I load what I can," Edward says. "What else can a person do?"

I don't know where they came from, but all of a sudden there are twenty or thirty people around the bakkie. Everyone is talking and gesticulating and asking Edward questions, as if they're at the scene of an accident and trying to establish what happened.

There are twenty-four chickens in the wire cage.

As I walk to the back of the bakkie, my cellphone rings. It's Pa again. He just wants to remind me to take photographs when I get to Daniëlskuil. "And remember, I'm sitting with you there in the car, son," he says before ringing off. "I'm with you all the time."

After a while, Daniël reappears from the house. The negotiations seem to have come to an end. He says something to Edward and some people start taking things down from the bakkie: a cupboard that's missing a door, a roll of bailing twine, an empty wooden cooldrink crate, two pot plants.

The woman with the colourful headscarf – Daniël's mother-in-law – watches everything. She's standing with her hands on her hips. She really doesn't feel like chatting.

She already has nine people living in her yard, but there's a corrugated-iron shack at the back of her house that she'll let Daniël and his family use. The word for this kind of hut is "makoekoe".

The people start carrying Daniël's family's belongings into the makoekoe.

Daniël carries a shoebox without a lid. It contains two biggish shells, a red candle, a small bottle of Red Star perfume, a Bee Gees tape, and a few papers with dirty fingerprints. "These are my pretty things, and my papers."

He puts the shoebox on the doorless cupboard that has already found a home in the corner of the hut. Ogies sniffs at the mattress on the floor. The child in Jessica's arms still hasn't made a sound. Outside the hut, Daniël's mother-in-law pulls a fifty rand note from her bra and asks a child to go and buy a bag of mealie meal from the shop.

A Hitachi hi-fi, a paraffin heater, a bottle of tomato sauce.

"At least we have a place again," says Daniël. "At least we can sleep at night."

One of the pot plants is standing on the floor next to the door. It looks like an elephant ear. I bend down and stick my finger into the soil in the pot. It's bone dry.

21.

At the café in Modderrivier on the other side of Jacobsdal, the day changes to dark grey when I see the *Volksblad* on the shelf:

LINDLEY. – "We killed them. We will be back . . ."

This is the terrifying message that was written in what is believed to be Sotho on a piece of cardboard, and left on the gate of the farm Tweefontein by the murderers of a three-year-old red-headed little girl and her parents.

The victims of the gruesome murders were Mr Attie Potgieter (40), his wife Wilna (36) and three-year-old Willemien. It is believed that Willemien was shot so that she would not be able to identify her parents' murderers.

Three farm workers have been arrested. Another two suspects were later arrested in townships in the area. According to information so far, one of them is just 17 years old.

The search for a sixth suspect continued yesterday evening.

The Potgieters were murdered on their eleventh wedding anniversary.

22.

The Star of the West in Kimberley is one of the oldest bars in the country. It's said that it served its first drink in 1870 and the oom on the bar stool next to me looks as if he could have been there that evening. He's been holding a glass of Jameson's for I don't know how long, his shoulders hunched up under a check jacket that's stretched out of shape from carrying heavy stuff in the pockets. A small cloth hat on his head. Bushy eyebrows.

The Formula 1 Hotel in Dutoitspan Road is where I found a place to sleep for the night. A special offer: R240 per room, no peppermint or lollipop on the bed. Everything is so cramped that it's possible to sit on the toilet and have a shower while I brush my teeth at the basin, adjust the TV, read the Gideon Bible on the bed, take clean clothes from my suitcase and wipe some of the dust from my shoes with the bedspread – all at the same time.

The bar section of the Star, where we're sitting at the counter, is packed with people – mostly men. It's dark outside. The television against the wall is showing a repeat broadcast of the third day's play in a 2001 test match between England and Australia. Or something like that.

There's an Oude Meester bust on the shelf, and this one, like so many others in so many bars around the country, is wearing a scarf (Springbok) around his neck, a cap (Blue Bulls) on his head, and sunglasses (Made in China).

There are only two women among all the men. One is smoking a thin cigarette. Or rather, she's not exactly smoking it; she's holding it pinched between her index and middle finger, away from her body, her wrist limp. Why do women always sit like this with a cigarette in a bar?

Both women are drinking Brutal Fruit. Pink. From the bottle.

It's difficult to tell, but most of the men seem to be drinking the Big Six: brandy, whisky, vodka, rum, cane and gin. A few are drinking beer, but they're mostly younger guys who've come straight from the office and are still wearing their lounge shirts, Edgars trousers and pointy shoes. Hardly any of the Big Six drinkers are wearing office clothes.

A few moments ago, three guys arrived, middle-aged and slightly overweight. Two are wearing two-toned khaki shirts, green ones. The third is wearing a Jeep T-shirt. It looks as if they're on their way to a hunt somewhere, or they're farmers in town to attend an auction tomorrow. They're drinking brandy and Coke Lite. A fat brandy drinker will almost always mix it with Coke Lite. A thin one drinks it with Coke.

One of the three brandy drinkers – the one in the Jeep T-shirt – is laughing loudly at something. The other two are laughing too. Brandy drinkers can be a happy bunch. A brandy drinker tends to hold his glass in front of him against his stomach, as if trying to hide his stomach behind the glass. Just like these three are doing now.

It's not something a cane drinker, like the guy with the thin beard two stools down, is likely to do. Between sips, a cane drinker rather puts his glass down on the counter. That's because most cane drinkers usually drink sitting down.

A brandy drinker prefers to drink standing up. He's usually also the first one to scold the bar girl about the music in the bar. "Take that rubbish off now," he'll call out after the third double Klipdrift. "Play 'De la Rey' for us." But it's not the brandy drinkers who sing along the loudest to songs like "De la Rey". It's the rum drinkers.

I haven't spotted a rum drinker here yet; perhaps it's too early for them.

Rum drinkers, I've noticed, tend to be more aggressive than

brandy drinkers. Don't get me wrong, brandy drinkers can be aggressive too, but their aggression is more often than not aimed at larger groups: blacks in general, or Western Province supporters, or plumbers, or some other random group.

But smile at a rum drinker's girlfriend and see what happens. He'll glare and glare and glare at you, and then you'd better leave the bar if you don't want to get hurt.

Rum drinkers who drink their rum with Cream Soda or Sparberry are particularly dangerous.

There's only one vodka drinker in the Star – or at least, I've only seen one here this evening. He's standing at a high bar table and doesn't take his eyes off the third day's cricket between England and Australia in who-knows-what-year. Vodka drinkers can be aggressive too, but they usually pass out before they hit you. Or they forget why they wanted to hit you in the first place and buy you a vodka so you can forget too.

Gin drinkers are the most peaceful of the lot, but I doubt whether the Star of the West gets to see many of them. They prefer to hang out at the exclusive De Beers Club. Gin drinkers don't laugh easily. A brandy drinker laughs the most, like the three over there. Tell him the silliest joke and he'll laugh. Late at night, a brandy drinker will also tell you Tolla van der Merwe stories and pretend they're his. A cane drinker isn't one for telling stories. Cane drinkers often sit on their own and mutter to themselves.

Whisky drinkers, on the other hand, like to tell one another things that cane drinkers would only mutter under their breath. Whisky drinkers would like to be deep. A whisky drinker also holds his glass against his chest, in the middle, as if trying to hide his heart.

A whisky drinker's glass is always half empty, never half full.

Much later that evening, the man next to me starts talking. He's British, Harry Frost, an engineer who came to Kimberley as a contract worker for the De Beers mining group more than twenty years ago. His wife died here, so he stayed here in Kimberley.

"Where are you off to?" he asks as I get ready to leave.

"Free State. A town called Lindley."

23.

When I got back to the Formula 1 Hotel from the Star of the West last night, I had five missed calls from Pa. My cellphone was in my trouser pocket and I didn't hear it. Now it's just after six in the morning.

I shower, dress, pack and get into the bakkie. By the time the sun comes up, I'm close to Brandfort, on my way to Lindley. There's a row of herons on a water trough near a corrugated-iron dam and a windmill. A farm signpost flashes by. I can't quite see what it says, but it looks like Goedgeluk.

More and more signposts come at me in the dawn. The world around here, like so many places in the country, speaks Afrikaans: Holpan, Skuinsdrift, Bossiekom.

My phone rings in the nook next to the gear lever. It's Pa, I just know it. Before I can greet him properly, he says: "Where are you, son? I'm worried sick about you." He doesn't sound like someone who isn't well.

I didn't hear my phone, I say. Sorry.

"Have you seen the news?" he asks.

"Does Pa mean the farm murder outside Lindley?"

"They want the farmers off the farms, son. They want our land."

"I'm on my way there, Pa. To Lindley."

"To Lindley?"

"Yes."

"What about Daniëlskuil?"

"I've decided to go to Lindley instead."

"But I thought you said you were going to Daniëlskuil."

"I *did* say I was going to Daniëlskuil, Pa. But now I'm going to Lindley."

"To do what?"

"I just want to have a look, Pa."

"Look at what?"

"At what's happening. I'm tired of having the newspapers and television tell me what's going on."

"So you're not going to Daniëlskuil any more?

"No."

"But son, I asked you so nicely to take photos of Daniëlskuil for me. Your pa was so looking forward to it."

He sounds hurt when he says goodbye. I put the phone back in the nook next to the gear leaver and drive on, trying not to think of Pa and instead explaining to myself the things I see next to the road: the entrance to a farm says something about the owner of the farm. Just look at a gate and it already tells you something: Goedgeluk's gate hangs level between two newish tarred poles and is kept shut with a chain – not a piece of wire. And there's no rust on the chain. Goedgeluk's owner must be a thorough man with a new pair of Cape Union Mart khaki trousers, and his yard doesn't look like a retirement home for worn-out tractors and farming implements.

If the gate is lopsided and the chain rusty, chances are the owner will walk over to greet you in washed-out rugby shorts and a pair of Nugget-hungry boots. A gate that can no longer open or close means you'll probably have to wait quite a while in the yard, with only the hen sitting on seven eggs in a hollow near the back door for company before the owner appears at the screen door with his hair mussed from sleeping.

Farm entrances here in the Free State are also very different to those in, say, the Boland. A white wall and a bed of gladioli next to the road, something you often see in the Boland, won't do here. The deeper you travel into the interior, the more bare the farm entrances become. Often there's just a gate with a modest Christian-national signpost like the one I just drove past: Klipbank.

It's as if the farmer wants to say: I'm too busy trying to survive here, I don't have time for show.

And all those who like to say that male farmers are chauvinists at heart should come here and see how many signposts display the name of the farmer's wife too: Gert and Rossie van Wyk. Piet and Tinkie Uys. Bernardus and Marina Nel.

In the Karoo you may see the painted outline of a sheep on a signpost, or if the farmer breeds horses, the signpost will be in the shape of a prancing horse with a wild mane. Here in the Free State, the crop farmers like to hang an old hand plough from a pole, and then they hang the signpost from that.

Everywhere you go, these signposts appear like small monuments to the hand plough and the ploughshare, the Lister engine or the Vaaljapie tractor, parked permanently at the gate.

The other side of Brandfort, a name jumps out at me from far off. The signpost is next to the road: De Aap. I stop next to it and get out. In the distance I see the farmhouse among big trees. This is where we – my pa and my ma and I – often stopped when we drove from Daniëlskuil to Natal to holiday with my oupa and ouma. This is where we stood and ate padkos, and I drank coffee from the awkward plastic cup that fitted over the colourful flask's lid. Ma always packed proper mugs for her and Pa, but I got that plastic cup that always burnt my hand because the ear was too small to put my finger through.

Pa and Ma and I stood in this spot and stared at the farmhouse in the distance. In those days it belonged to State President C.R. Swart, or, as we called him, oom Blackie – oom Blackie and tannie Nellie. As if we knew them personally. Pa, Pa, Pa.

I fetch the cellphone from the bakkie and dial his number. Dammit, why does he always manage to make me feel guilty?

I hear his phone ring and ring, then the scraping and scratching, and then the "Hello . . . Hello". His voice is old and tired. "Is that you, son?" he asks.

"I just wanted to say I'm sorry I'm not going to Daniëlskuil any more, Pa."

"That's okay, son. Do as you see fit." Silence. "Your pa is going to stay in bed today. Your pa isn't feeling well."

Once I'm on the road again, I notice that here, too, on the road between Brandfort and Lindley, like everywhere else in the country, there are neglected farm gates. The sign is skew and rusty, or it's no longer there. The gate is half-hidden behind grass and locked with a chain and a padlock.

But if you take a closer look you'll see that a gate like this is usually not far from the ruins of a farmyard. The owner has died or has moved away to retire, and a farmer who already has a farm-house of his own to live in – or some or other trust or company – has taken over the farm, just for the land, for the grazing or the fields.

On the other side of Winburg, numbers start to appear on the name boards, numbers that gleam in the night: Biesieput A553. Name boards with numbers like these have become a common sight.

Farmers will soon be able to get new name boards that will allow the police to respond quickly to complaints, says an article that I tore from a community newspaper in the platteland not too long ago. *The idea of having a name board with an identification number for each farm arose because so many farm names have changed since so many have changed owners lately.*

Everywhere you go, you also see signs of farm watch organisa-tions and security companies at farm gates. I passed one that stated: *Here we live under the protecting hand of Jesus Christ. Nela Roux.*

About twenty kilometres on the other side of Lindley I see an avenue of tall bluegum trees next to the road. There's no signpost. I stop. The gate is open and there's a sign with a warning next to one of the gate posts: *Geen ingang. No entry. Ha ho kenwe.* The farm-house sits on a rise. Nothing moves in the yard.

It's Tweefontein, the farm where the Potgieters were murdered.

Perhaps I should first see what's going on in the town, I decide.

The bakkie's window is open. I can smell the bluegums and I can hear them. A bluegum tree is never silent. Its leaves are constantly rustling. Even if there's hardly a wind, like now, you can hear the whisper of its leaves.

24.

Koos Gerber is standing outside the Engen garage in Lindley in the Free State, waving an angry finger. "That's why I say they should bring back the death penalty," he says. "It's the only thing that will help. Hang the buggers who do these things." He looks at Petrus Makwena, the petrol attendant who is filling up his Toyota Fortuner. "What do you say, baba? Or are you one of Malema's people too?"

Petrus keeps his head down and keeps quiet. He's been a petrol attendant in Lindley for thirty-three years.

Koos's wife Linda comes towards us from the café holding two Red Bulls. The Gerbers are from Pretoria, and are on their way to Clarens. But they decided to drive via Lindley after reading in the newspaper about the Potgieters' murder.

"We want to see where it happened," says Koos, getting back into the Fortuner. He slams his door shut, then Linda's slams shut, and the Fortuner is off while Petrus Makwena goes to sit on an upside-down cooldrink crate outside the attendants' office. Attie Potgieter and his Nissan bakkie were regular customers.

"This is a bad thing, Ntate. The farmers are angry. I hear they organised a meeting in Arlington." Petrus gives a whistle and shakes his head. "Eish."

One of the other attendants joins us. He's also heard that the local farmers are gathering in Arlington, the neighbouring town about eighteen kilometres away where Wilna Potgieter was the assistant manager at the co-op.

In the Spar down the road a notice warns:

No one wearing a blanket is allowed to enter.

Pretty much all I knew about Lindley before was that Dr Danie Craven, the rugby legend, was born and grew up here. I head for Arlington through open, hilly countryside with pans and streams and willow trees in the valleys.

Arlington is little more than a row of grain silos with a church, a few houses, and a rugby field, a co-op and a shop with a Coke advertisement on the wall outside.

A few bakkies are parked near the silos – farm bakkies splattered with mud. From somewhere, a voice is bellowing over a loud-speaker: "Gentlemen, I have five hundred for this water tank. I have five hundred. I have five hundred . . ."

It's the familiar voice of an auctioneer at an auction.

A group of men in farm clothes stand in an open area next to a water tank and other farm implements: a ripper and a cultivator and a trailer that's seen better days . . . "Gentlemen, I have six hundred. I have six hundred . . ."

A young girl walks over. "Would you like to register?" She holds a card out to me. If you write down your name and other details, you can join in the bidding. She points to an older man in a blue shirt. "They're selling oom Boet Schultz's things, oom."

Oom Boet is in his seventies and has farmed in the district for the past twenty-five years. But today he's selling everything. "I have four daughters and not one of their husbands wants to farm," he says after the hammer falls on an R800 bid for the water tank. "I can't blame them." He's quiet for a while. "This thing with the Potgieters shook us, my friend."

The auction couldn't be postponed because it had been adver-tised long ago.

"The people are confused." Oom Boet looks at the men around him. "You can see how tense they are."

"And now for the tractors, gentlemen!" calls the auctioneer, a tall man whose breast pocket is stuffed with pens and papers and things. He crosses the road and the farmers follow him in a sad procession. None of the anger or even the bravado portrayed in the newspapers is to be seen anywhere here.

Dirk van Rensburg, a prominent farmer in the area and a former mayor of Arlington, is among them. He points to the church down the road. "They were confirmed in that church," he says. "Willemien was christened there."

Dirk, who is an elder, tells me how, for years, the community paid old moruti Rampolo, a lay preacher, to minister to the farm folk around here. But moruti Rampolo died at the beginning of the year. They also recently organised a Nehemia Bible study course for the people of the local township.

A man dressed in jeans and Crocs walks past. "Dominee!" oom Dirk calls to him. "Dominee!"

Dominee Piet Taljaard, the Dutch Reformed minister, is at the auction too. Dominee Piet comes closer, and I realise for the umpteenth time this morning that a murder like that of the Potgieters is something that defies words. Everyone manages superficial words about being shocked or angry, but what we really feel is so much more.

"The murders aren't good for us," says dominee Piet. "It's not good for us . . ." He searches for words. "The people have begun asking me questions that I don't always know how to answer."

Should one really love others as you love yourself? Are you allowed to take revenge? Those kinds of questions.

This morning dominee Piet went to fetch milk at a nearby farm, and when he arrived a woman embraced him and started to cry.

The auctioneer takes up position near a row of tractors. Oom Boet is there too. He stands with his hands folded, contemplating the tractors as if they're old friends he'll never see again. "Where's the driver for this tractor?" shouts the auctioneer as he points to an early-model John Deere.

"Driver!" someone shouts. "Driver!"

A man appears. He's Daniël Moheli, who has worked for oom Boet for over thirty years. Like many of the farmers, Daniël's also wearing a khaki shirt with green patches on the shoulders and pockets.

Daniël gets up on the tractor.

"Right, start it for us!" calls the auctioneer.

Daniël starts the tractor and revs the engine before turning it off again.

"I have thirty thousand! Gentleman," his voice reverberates, "I have thirty thousand!"

Daniël gets down from the tractor. Oom Boet is going to retire in Bethlehem, but Daniël doesn't know what's going to become of him. "Baas Boet hasn't told us anything," he says. "I think he'll take care of us. He's a good baas."

Daniël, who has an old Nissan car, also knew Wilna Potgieter who worked at the co-op for years. "He helped me a lot, that miesies," he says. "If I needed something for my car, I went to him. Last week he ordered brake pads and an oil filter for me."

I walk over to the co-op around the corner. Danie Marx, the manager, fumbles for words and then looks as if he's about to cry. He points to the back of the shop where there's a cubicle with a desk and a computer. It used to be Wilna's office.

The desk is clean and tidy. Next to the computer monitor is a cloth sunflower in a little bottle. There's also a card that reads: *Trust in the Lord.*

Koos and Linda Gerber, whom I'd seen earlier at the Engen in Lindley, have just pulled up outside the Arlington shop opposite the silos. They did go to Tweefontein, where the Potgieters were murdered. "There's nothing there," says Koos, a quantity surveyor. "All that's left in the yard is a little Jack Russell."

The auction of oom Boet Schultz's remaining farm equipment is still in full swing. "I have one thousand, gentlemen. I have one thousand!" the auctioneer booms at the handful of sombre farmers gathered around him. At this moment it looks like an auction for a lifestyle rather than an old Soilmaster planter.

"Dirk, have you heard?" Leon Bobbert asks oom Dirk van Rensburg, who is still here. "It was on the radio just now: there was another farm murder in the Western Transvaal. They beat a woman to death with a hammer."

Chris and Marthie Erasmus were attacked on their farm near Koster the previous afternoon.

As we're standing here next to the silos, I can almost see the words moving through the air from farmer to farmer. "Have you heard? A woman in Koster was beaten to death with a hammer? Have you heard . . ."

The clouds hang low over the town. It looks as if it might rain.

"Do you see that man over there?" whispers a woman. "He was the one who found the Potgieters' bodies." She points to a man with a beard who is standing next to a plough and listening to the auctioneer.

The man's name is Henk Human and he was the Potgieters' neighbour. When he arrived at Tweefontein's farmyard yesterday . . . "I don't want to talk about it," says Henk and looks at his hands. "What happened was God's will."

Henk leads me aside. "I don't want to talk about it," he repeats. "I washed their blood off the floor this morning."

He doesn't want to talk about it, yet you can see that he wants to talk about it. "Let me put it this way: I'm not against the new South Africa. Things would have been a lot worse if it was still the old South Africa. A lot worse. A lot. There would have been even more murders." He's quiet for a while, almost as if he has surprised himself with the words that have came out of his mouth. "I was in the army, in Angola. I'd rather live here than go back to Angola ever again."

Henk walks off. Oom Dirk comes back. He and oom Leon Bobbert want to show me the church and farmers' association hall and the club. It's as if they want to say, come and see for yourself, this is who we are. Do we deserve what happened here?

At the club there's a painting of Doc Craven because Doc really did come from Arlington. Pinkie Craven, who's related to Doc, still farms here. Doc played his first match on the rugby pitch outside, which is now criss-crossed with footpaths.

A framed certificate hangs on another wall. Part of it reads: *Thank you, South Africa. Your goodwill gives Rhodesia strength.*

The people of the city of Buluwayo gave the certificate to the local farmers years ago when they donated fuel to Rhodesians who were suffering under international sanctions.

Sometime in the afternoon I drive back to Tweefontein.

Geen ingang, a sign at the gate still warns. *No entry. Ha ho kenwe.* The bluegums are still having whispered conversations.

Three of the murderers who were arrested had worked on the farm; the other three are from the township in the dorp.

The yard mirrors countless others. To the right there's an avenue of pine trees. The house is built of stone and surrounded by lawn. A rain gauge hangs from a pole. A few Frieslands are grazing in a paddock. There are no people around.

There are window boxes with violets and sweetpeas everywhere. Attie's white bakkie is standing under a trellis and has powder the police use to detect fingerprints on the windows. This is where the Potgieters came to a stop for the last time. According to the newspaper, Willemien was wearing a pink ribbon in her hair when she was shot.

A Jack Russell appears from behind the bakkie. He doesn't bark or jump up against me, which is unusual for a Jack Russell. He runs away when I come closer. It takes me about fifteen minutes to find him in his hiding place in a ditch behind the house.

Louisa Naudé, Wilna Potgieter's sister, and her husband Ruan arrive. They're coming to give milk to the hand-reared calves.

Louisa points to the dog in my arms. "That's Vlekkie, Willemien's little dog."

25.

The afternoon light is fading when I arrive at Steynsrus, about half an hour's drive from the Potgieters' farm. I'm looking for somewhere to sleep. It's been a long day.

The town is looking tired. There's a Top Furnishers and three cafés. At the top of the main street is the Dutch Reformed church, a sandstone building behind a palisade fence with sharp points.

The gate is open. On the spur of the moment I drive in. I haven't been in a church in a long time. I need the dignified silence of a church right now.

A worker is weeding a bed of cannas. I go over to talk to him. He says the side door is open.

The building, says the cornerstone, was designed by Gerard Moerdijk:

Laid in honour of God
by
Rev. J.R. Alheit
On the 7th of April 1928

Architect: Gerard Moerdijk   Contractor: C.V. Spalding

I open the door and go inside. The smell of floor polish and furniture polish and dust in the organ pipes accompanies me down the aisle.

The light – the first thing to strike me in a church is always the light. Or perhaps it's the lack of light, because churches like this one often have stained-glass windows. Even during the day it's always yellowy-dusk in here. For some, an old Dutch Reformed church is too sombre, too old-worldly, too austere and pious. This is exactly what I am looking for, because it's the dark corners inside myself that are worrying me.

The parquet floor in front of the pulpit is covered with a grey carpet where the communion table and baptismal font are positioned. The wooden blocks are reddish-brown, with an ivory-coloured one here and there. They are the most noticeable, the ivory-coloured ones. The rest is just floor.

I go to the vestry, a rectangular room with high windows, as if the architect wanted to make sure that no one could see in from the outside, or out from the inside. Close to the wall, on the pulpit side of the room, a long table with round legs stands gleaming. Chairs are arranged against the other three walls. Above the chairs are portraits of all the congregation's previous ministers: dominee J.H. Alheit, dominee Adriaan Janse van Rensburg, dominee Daan Malan . . . The ones from long ago are wearing bow ties and the more recent ones wear white ties. One of the most recent ones, dominee Quintes Scholtz, is wearing an open-necked shirt without a tie.

On the table lies a stack of calendars with a photograph of the church on them. The caption above the photograph says *Dutch Reformed Church Steynsrus 2010*. Next to the photographs are the addresses and telephone numbers of the dominee, the church secretary, the verger and the organist.

I leave the vestry and go back into the church. There's a red velvet cloth with gold tassels on the communion table, and on it lies a Bible that's closed with two golden latches. Next to the Bible are a silver communion cup and a silver platter.

In a church like this it's impossible to forget that your soul is very old.

There's a staircase on either side of the pulpit, and all you can see from below is part of a chair's backrest sticking out above the pulpit.

The pulpit cloth is red with gold lettering:

THE LORD

COMETH

The wooden benches are upright and narrow. I pass through the yellow dusk and sit down when I reach the bench at the front. I can see the sharp points of the palisade fence through the open side door.

Should you really love everyone as yourself? I wonder. Is one allowed to take revenge? The bench's legs and joints and seams creak under me, and then, as if a fatherly hand is gently pushing me from behind, my head bows and my eyes close.

26.

On the way from Steynsrus to Kroonstad my phone rings and the word "Pa" flashes on the small screen. I answer, but it's Johannes Bogotsi on the other end. He's phoning from Pa's cellphone and says: "Ouboet says I must ask you where you are now."

"Is Ouboet all right, Johannes?" I ask. "Doesn't he want to speak to me?"

"Ouboet is lying down, but he's all right. I rubbed his feet with the medicine. He doesn't want to talk now."

I can hear Pa's voice in the background. He says something to Johannes. Then Johannes comes back on the phone: "Ouboet wants to know where you are."

Does Pa think I'll decide to go to Daniëlskuil after all because I feel guilty?

"Tell Ouboet I'm still on the road," I say, "but I think I'll look for somewhere to sleep in Kroonstad."

"Kroonstad?"

"Yes. Kroonstad."

"Kroonstad," he repeats, maybe so that he won't forget.

"And tomorrow or the day after I'm going to Pietersburg. Polokwane. I want to see where Julius Malema comes from."

"Malema?" Johannes laughs.

"Tell Ouboet I'm going to Malema's place tomorrow or the day after."

Perhaps it's because I've heard and read Malema's name too often these last few days: Malema, Malema, Malema. On television and the radio, in the newspaper. At the petrol station in Lindley. At the café in Steynsrus. Malema, Malema, Malema.

Whites who use the name do it with a certain respect. Or is it fear? Or distaste? Or could it be loathing?

It's as if Julius Malema is no longer just a person. People see him as the symbol of a younger generation that grew up in townships.

Malema is a word that bends under the weight of the future and of what could still happen in this country.

I read somewhere that he grew up in Masakeng, a township near Polokwane. That's where I want to go.

If it's possible to record and document nostalgia, why can't you do the same with your fears too? The longer I'm on the road, the more it feels as if that might be a cure for the strange feeling the country sometimes gives me.

27.

After spending the night in one of the guest rooms behind the Ultra
City outside Kroonstad, I continue driving north in the morning. I
take a back road because I first want to see Kitte Honiball in Vanderbijlpark.

In a sense, Kitte and those like Kitte are the exact opposite of
Malema and those like him. Malema and those like him have ex-
pectations of wealth and economic freedom; Kitte and those like
him have more or less made peace with poverty and hardship and
displacement.

Not far from Kroonstad, I encounter the first serious potholes
since leaving Cape Town. Deep ones. Lots of them. Here and there I
have to leave the road and drive on the gravel shoulder to avoid the
really deep ones.

Since yesterday I've been wondering what exactly it is that I'm
seeing around me. It's as if the country becomes more and more
sullen and impenetrable the further north I go. Pavements in Free
State dorps are dirtier than those in the Northern and Western
Cape. There are fences with sharp teeth around the churches. There
are bullet holes in the road signs.

In Heilbron I want to put some diesel in the bakkie. There are a
few of us waiting in line at the Caltex filling station. A minibus
comes past, the driver's arm clamped tightly over the door. It
squeezes in between a guy in a Peugeot and me. *The Bold and the
Beautiful* is written on its rear window. The guy in the Peugeot gestures but doesn't get out. The taxi driver's arm remains clamped
over the door.

A woman is standing next to her car, talking loudly. Across the roofs of cars driving past she's having a conversation with a man on the other side of the street. A child is sitting on a step, chewing on a cooked chicken leg. What do they call it again? A runaway.

In a shop window I see a notice informing the people of Heilbron that an aerobics class will be held every weekday from 07:30 until 08:30 and from 17:00 until 18:00 in the old stone church. The old jukskei club building has been taken over by the Heilbron Gymnasium.

A Nissan Sentra pulls up in front of the café. A small dog wearing a Blue Bulls jacket lies in the back window.

The potholes in the main street have been filled with earth, but no one has come to flatten it with a roller. In some places there are rocks in the middle of the road. Down the road, a sign on a garden gate warns:

> Rottweiler aan diens. Pasop!
> Rottweiler on duty. Beware!

Throughout the country, the good old garden gate is disappearing and changing. Most new homes don't even have a garden gate. Often there's just one big electric gate that slides open to let you drive into the yard where you can get out of your car, protected by a wall or a fence.

At some security complexes the homes have a front or side gate, but can you really call that low little thing that barely comes up to your knees a garden gate?

Once upon a time, twenty, thirty years ago, the garden gate was the gateway to most homes in an ordinary neighbourhood. Usually it was painted silver and waited for you at the start of a cement footpath that took you straight to the front door.

In those days, fences and gates had only two sorts of signs. One indicating that the yard had its own borehole, and the other the familiar: *Pasop vir die hond*. Sometimes repeated in English: *Beware of the dog*. Even when there were two or three dangerous dogs in the yard, the sign still said: *Beware of the dog*. Singular.

In time, it's as if a simple "Pasop vir die hond/Beware of the dog" on the gate wasn't enough any more. Beware-of-the-dog signs took on a completely different meaning. A home owner used to put it up on the gate because he was afraid his dog may bite someone, but now the notice has taken on the role of deterrent. It's as though many home owners don't want prospective trespassers to think for a second that their dog could be an overweight labrador or a temperamental mutt in a Blue Bulls jacket.

The evolution of the beware-of-the-dog sign says something about how powerless and desperate crime and violence make people feel.

At first a black language joined the Afrikaans and English on the sign. Some gates now read: *Pasop vir die hond / Beware of the dog / Qaphela Hlokomela*. But after a while, it seems, people started to think even this wasn't enough of a deterrent. Signs identifying a specific breed started to make their appearance: *Beware of the bull terrier. Beware of the boerbull . . .*

Some gates also began warning: *Beware of the dogs.* Plural.

The *pasop/beware* was no longer aggressive enough either. It became: *Beware of the dogs. Enter and be eaten.* Or: *I am on guard*, accompanied by a picture of an angry dog.

But often, very often, it was still the same dog or dogs in the yard: Vlooi or Yster or Tyson or Leeu. It was still the same home owner too, who had just become more afraid of a break-in or robbery and so adapted the sign on the gate.

Sometimes you even see a sign that warns: *Beware this property is guarded by snakes / Lumkela ezi sakhiwo sikuhuselwe zunyoka.*

And then there are the signs you should fear most: *Never mind the dog, beware of the owner.* These often bear the image of a man taking aim with a pistol, straight at you, irrespective of who you are.

28.

There's something wrong with Kitte's cellphone, because I can't get hold of him. And we did agree: eleven o'clock. Almost an hour has passed since I began looking for him on the smallholdings – plots, Kitte calls them – here on the outskirts of Vanderbijlpark.

Every time I call, I get his voicemail – it's not a very smooth message. It sounds as if he got someone to help him when he recorded it because I can hear a man's voice in the background: "You must speak now, Kitte. Say you're not available." Then Kitte's voice: "Oh." Only then does his voicemail message come on: "Hello, this is Kitte. I'm not available right now. Please call again."

At the moment he's living with someone called Sewes on a plot somewhere between the Golden Highway and the old Potchefstroom road, between Vanderbijlpark and Sebokeng. Just before I get to Olga Kirsch Street, he said, I should turn left and continue until I get to Fred Drotské. At the third plot I should turn right and carry on a little. Sewes's plot "has a helluva big syringa tree next to the gate. You can't miss it, pal".

There's no such tree anywhere. Eventually I'm back in Olga Kirsch. Who would have decided to name a street here, among the plots, after Olga Kirsch, the poet who wrote finely-wrought Afrikaans poems about womanhood and religion? It's not as if the other streets around here are named after poets. There's a Moshoeshoe Street, a Houtkop Street and a Skippie Botha Street.

I can tell that many of the homes must have been grand in the seventies. The stoeps are slate and the roofs are tiled. But the original owners no longer live here, maybe because Sebokeng sprang up nearby. I stop outside one of the houses. The gutter at the front has sagged and hangs in front of a window, the garage door is stuck at an angle in the door frame, the sitting-room window has a crack that somebody tried to fix with sticking plaster. On the patchy lawn a child's bicycle and a punctured plastic ball lie amid a minefield of dog turds.

Somewhere inside the house a dog is barking like mad.

A man opens the front door, sidles out and closes it behind him. His jeans are hanging halfway down his bum. The dog carries on barking. The man turns around. "Fuck off, Tyson!" he shouts at the house. "Fuck off!"

The dog is quiet for a few seconds, then starts barking again.

"Ma, tell that fuckin' dog to shut up!"

Almost instantly the barking stops.

The man comes to stand in front of me. He has a few days' stubble on his cheeks and a lifetime of despair in his eyes. Tiny Fouché. "No, oh hell, my chom," he replies when I ask about Kitte. "No, sorry. There are sixteen of us living here but he's not here."

29.

Over fifty thousand poor whites live in squatter camps, shelters and other hovels in Gauteng.

30.

Maybe more streets here were named after poets, but the signs have just disappeared? I head back in the direction of Olga Kirsch, along streets where ditches run like the lines of a poem on a blank page. In the distance, the grey of Johannesburg hangs in the air. The grey land.

My phone rings and Pa's name appears on the screen, but who will it be this time, him or Johannes?

It's Pa. His voice is faltering and weak. "Morning, son. Where are you?"

I tell him.

"Johannes says you're on your way to Pietersburg. To Malema."

"That's right, Pa. I want to see where he grew up."

"Why, son?"

"I just want to see it, Pa. He has to come from somewhere too. I want to try and understand why he's the way he is."

"He is a little troublemaker, son. He's still going to cause big problems." A dog barks in the background. It sounds like Brakkenjan, Pa's Jack Russell. Pa's quiet for quite a while and then he says: "So, you're not going to Daniëlskuil any more?"

"No, Pa." I say it slowly and as calmly as possible.

"But you're going to Malema?"

"Yes, Pa."

"What do you have against Daniëlskuil?"

"Nothing, Pa."

"So why don't you want to go there any more? You said you wanted to."

"I don't want to go any more, Pa. Daniëlskuil is finished. It's in the past."

"Wasn't it good enough? Didn't you like living there?"

"I did like living there, Pa. I just don't want to go there and take photos and get nostalgic over something that's no longer the way I thought it was."

"What are you talking about, son?"

"The past wasn't better than today, Pa. I'm fed up with people, myself included, who can't stop yearning for the past. That's what's making us feel out of place in our own country."

"But didn't we have good things in the past too? Were we bad through and through?"

"We weren't all bad, Pa. But our longing for the past is so strong it's making us believe we're innocent."

"Why are you so serious lately, son? That's not how Pa knows you. Pa is worried about you."

"Stop bloody worrying about me, Pa! I'm just as worried about you!"

Pa says nothing – not immediately. When he speaks again, all he says is: "I didn't know that's how you felt, son. Do as you think fit. You always know better."

"And bloody well stop saying I always know better, Pa!"

I return to the old Potch road and then turn off onto a gravel road leading back to the plots. Strange. At many of the houses life is clearly a struggle, yet things are simply scattered around the bare lawn: toys, car parts, broken furniture.

Somehow, I end up in Skippie Botha Street again. It feels like a kind of Bermuda Triangle that swallows up people's dignity. A man is walking next to the road, pulling a cart with a car battery on it.

Someone is running towards me across a piece of open land. I'll be damned! It's Kitte! He must have recognised my bakkie. I stop next to the road. He stops in front of me with clothes that hang on him like a scarecrow's. He hasn't shaved in days, and his eyes are red with the smoke of many nights next to a fire in the open. "Sorry, chom. My phone's giving trouble. I dropped it in the toilet."

Another guy comes over. "This is my chom, Johan Beneke."

We drive to Sewes's house and there it's the same story. The place was grand once upon a time, but now it's all sagging gutters and cracked windows.

There's a tent behind the house, and Kitte and Johan have been living in it for over a month. A smallish cart is parked in front of the tent. Nearby lies one of those surfboard-type things that has sails.

Kitte has built the cart himself and now uses it to travel all over the country. He used to pull it behind a Honda 90-cc motorbike, but he swapped the Honda for a Kawasaki 650-cc in Theunissen in the Free State and the Kawa never really wanted to go. Now he pushes the cart wherever he wants, with the tent, windsurfer and all his earthly belongings on it.

Kitte can't stop moving from one place to another. Call him a drifter, even call him unemployed, but don't call him a tramp. "A tramp is someone who has run out of plans. I'm more like a cowboy." He looks at Johan. "We're cowboys, aren't we, Johan?"

Johan nods but says nothing.

The name on Kitte's birth certificate is Johannes Bernardus Honiball. But no one calls him that. He was born in Johannesburg, one of nine children. Later he was sent to an orphanage in Ugie in the Eastern Cape. Still later he got a job as a stoker but then one day he was in a car accident with another guy in a Chev Firenza. That's when Kitte began his never-ending drifting.

Now, at fifty-three, he's somewhat of a legend. People stop next to the road to take photos of him and his cart and the windsurfer that he drags around with him like a dream wherever he goes. Apparently OFM, a Free State radio station, even interviewed him some time ago.

"I talked to OFM over the phone. Just like that." Kitte holds up his cellphone. "The presenter asked: 'Mister Honiball, tell the listeners about all the things you have on your cart.' So I said: 'Well, I have a windsurfer, I have a fishing rod, I have pots and pans ..."

The windsurfer on the ground next to the tent isn't the one he had way back when I first met him. At the time, he was on his way to Port Elizabeth with his little dog, Boetie.

"I left that windsurfer in Middelburg in the Eastern Cape. Some guy wanted to give Boetie and me a lift. When he saw the windsurfer, he said: 'I don't have room for that thing, mate.' So I ran to the police station. 'Here's a windsurfer for you guys,' I said to the constable. 'You can make a book shelf or something with it.' Kitte shakes his head. "Can you believe it, that constable says to me: 'We don't want that thing, Meneer.' So I threw the windsurfer on their lawn and shouted at them: 'Then here's a statue for you, Constable!'"

In PE he worked for a while with his brother-in-law, John, a professional fisherman. He also spent Christmas with John Palm and his family. "I don't really drink but I drank a little something because it was Christmas. I didn't want to feel out of place."

But a month or so after that, Kitte came here to Vanderbijl. "John Palm said: 'Kitte, I'm putting you on the bus back today.' Then I said to John's little girl: 'Marlies, you take Boetie. I'm not allowed to take him on the bus.'"

Johan Beneke hasn't moved in all this time and listens to every word Kitte says, as if it's a lecture he's attending. He hasn't been drifting for much more than a year.

Back in Vanderbijl, Kitte began working at oom Joggie Pieterse's gardening service. "I serviced the lawn mowers. I'm an ace mechanic."

But then oom Joggie died unexpectedly and Sewes gave him a temporary place to stay. Sewes also gave him the windsurfer.

"Sewes cleans people's yards, and you know what rich people are like: as soon as something isn't new any more, they throw it away. So Sewes gave me the windsurfer."

Kitte points to Johan Beneke. "Tell him about yourself, Johan."

"I got divorced, so I took to the road," says Johan. "I've travelled from Pretoria down to Upington and back again. I've also been to

Pietersburg and back and to PE and to Knysna and to Bloemfontein and back."

Kitte smiles, almost a proud smile. "This is the kind of man I want with me." Suddenly his cellphone begins to beep. It's an SMS from his brother Dries. It's eight years to the day since they buried their other brother Jan. "Here, read this." Kitte passes me his cellphone.

Today is eight yrs since Jan's funeral. Th world is a shit place. You strugle, then death comes for you. Your brother. Dries.

"Where's Dries, Kitte?" asks Johan.

"Ellisras. Now that place is something else, my friend."

Kitte walks back to the bakkie with me. He wants to know where I've been because the bakkie is covered in dust. He knows about the Potgieters' murder. "It's all that Malema's doing," he says. "That guy, he's going to cause lots of problems for us."

31.

On the N1, between Pienaarsrivier and the Kranskop tollgate, Johannes Bogotsi calls, this time from his cellphone. "Yes, Johannes," I say. "What is it now? What does Ouboet want?"

"I don't phone for Ouboet. I phone for myself."

"Where are you?" I ask.

"Here in the yard, in my room."

I can see him sitting in the room with the rust-coloured steel door in the yard behind the house. On the floor is a tattered flokati rug that once lay on Ma's side of the bed in the bedroom.

"What do you mean you're phoning for yourself, Johannes?"

"I want to talk to you."

"You can talk, Johannes."

"You mustn't fight with Ouboet. He is very good by me. He is good by all of us."

32.

On the other side of Kranskop I turn off the N1 and onto the R101, the so-called alternative route. Through Naboomspruit, which is now called Mookgopong, and Potgietersrus, which has become Mokopane.

Here Africa gets a hold of you. The rich smell of the bush wafts in through the bakkie's open window. In the dorps wild bananas grow in the gardens, and frangipanis, and bougainvilleas. At a cross-road a boy is selling bags of dried mopani worms.

A Nissan Laurel is lumbering along at sixty kilometres an hour. The painted letters on the back say "Defensive Driving School". "God is Great Spaza Shop," I read on a small flat-roofed building next to the road. "Thugs on horseback shoot and rape villagers," announces a *Daily Sun* poster hanging from a lamp post.

It's as if a different way of thinking is on the verge of establishing itself here.

At a filling station on the other side of Mokopane, far too many cars are waiting at its four petrol pumps. Two petrol attendants are shouting in confusion at each other, while a third calmly sits on a cooldrink crate and watches.

I get out, the sweat making my shirt stick to my back between my shoulder blades. In the fridge inside the café just a few luke-warm cans of Coke and a solitary can of Mirinda are to be found.

Outside on the pavement, music is blaring from a loudspeaker – music filled with guitars and rhythms trying to entice you to a place you're too scared to go to.

"We don't take petrol card," says the petrol attendant. "Our machine is broken."

It has something to do with Africa, this uneasy feeling that's growing in me as I drive north. This feeling that there's something going on in the streets and in people's minds and among people that could be dangerous. Or is Africa just the name we give to things we struggle to understand?

33.

Bongani Ramasala glowers at me. "He isn't Julius," he corrects me. "Julius is white people's name." He points to the small ramshackle houses around us. "Here, everyone calls him Sello."

Bongani is sitting on an empty beer crate in front of the Forget Me Not Spaza Shop in Masakeng, a township outside Polokwane. I stopped here just now because I'm lost. I'm looking for Masakeng, Zone 1, the place where the newspapers say Malema grew up.

Bongani's eyes are bloodshot. A Hansa quart waits at his feet. "What do you want to do to Malema?"

I've come in peace, I explain. I don't want to do anything to Malema. I just want to see what it looks like here where he was born and where I've heard his family still lives.

"Sello's place is at the flats." He points to a side street. "Go up there. You will see the flats. Just ask for the flats."

Apparently that's where Ma Malema, as Julius's grandmother is known around here, lives.

It's just after half past nine in the morning. Bongani picks up the Hansa and takes a big swig. I drive up the side street, through more potholes and over speed bumps, deeper and deeper into Masakakeng, but can't see a block of flats anywhere. On a corner I see a shop with flaky paint and flaky lettering: Corner Store. Two young guys are sitting on the front steps. They're wearing the same pointy shoes I've seen Malema wear in photographs. "Rampashane" is the shoes' township name.

Suddenly I feel as if my eyes are deceiving me. Diagonally opposite the Corner Store is a house that looks as if it doesn't belong here – a double storey behind a high wall and an electric gate. It stands there like a huge promise.

One of the young guys comes over, suspicious. "You look for something?"

"I'm looking for the flats."

"There." He points to the double-storey house.

"But it's a house."

"We call it 'the flats' because it's big like the flats."

At the gate, a guard in a black uniform peers out of a guard house. He flatly refuses: no one is allowed to see Ma Malema. At the small house next door on the right a tired Nissan bakkie is resting under an avo tree. The two youngsters in their rampashane follow me. Both are brimming with angry questions:

"Why are you here?"

"You're a white man, how can we trust you?"

"You don't like Malema because he don't keep quiet."

The front door of the small house – the one with the bakkie – swings open and an old grey-haired man appears. Thomas Baloi. He scolds the two guys and beckons me to come inside, have a seat. At first we speak English but then he says: "I speak Afferkaans." He also knows Julius as Sello.

Oom Thomas's wife, Irene, joins us. She's wearing a brown dress made from shweshwe. They have been the Malemas' neighbours for years. They watched Sello grow up, says oom Thomas.

It feels as though this isn't how things should be. That Malema shouldn't have a neighbour who can speak Afrikaans and who has a print of Da Vinci's *Last Supper* hanging in his sitting room. There's also a wall unit with a TV and a picture of a young Queen Elizabeth on it.

And among it all . . . oh, *there* it is – the empty Grünberger Stein bottle displayed like an ornament.

Oom Thomas points through the window to the big house next door. "Sello built these flats for his mother. Flora. He doesn't have brothers or sisters, he's the only one. As soon as the house was finished, he wanted to show Flora and say: 'Look here, my ma. I've built a house for you. Here's your room.' But then she lost her life, then she died."

Irene says something to him in Sotho.

"It was the falling sickness," oom Thomas says. "Flora died from the falling sickness."

Apparently Malema's mother suffered from severe epilepsy.

"Flora often came to visit. She sat just there. We'd talk nicely and laugh, and then I'd see her start to make like this." Thomas begins to twitch from head to toe. "Then her body would start to shake. Then we helped her to lie down and we held her.

"Other times, Sello would come and say: 'Oom, my mother is twitching again. She's sick. Come and help.'"

Malema lived here until about six years ago.

Oom Thomas points to the TV on the wall unit. "Sello is a big man now. We see him on the TV and say: 'That man comes from among us.' He didn't become naughty like the other young ones. He doesn't walk around at night and grab your money like them. He takes care of his grandmother."

Not that Malema was always a good child.

"He made his mother angry," says oom Thomas. "He told her he was going to school but then he didn't go to school. He hid until school was finished and then came back. His mother came to me and said: 'Talk to Sello.' So I called Sello but I didn't beat him. I talked to him nicely. 'Go to school,' I said to him. 'Don't be full of nonsense.'

"Another time, Sello just disappeared. We looked for him and we looked for him. Then he came back and said: 'I was in Jo'burg. I went to Chris Hani's funeral.'"

Malema was just thirteen in 1993 when he apparently took the bus to go to Hani's funeral. It was around the same time that Peter Mokaba, a former leader of the ANC Youth League who also came from Polokwane, regularly used the slogan "Kill the Boer, kill the farmer!" at meetings in the area. Freedom was in the air, and Flora and Ma Malema and people like Thomas couldn't keep Julius at home.

"All Sello wanted was to go to the politics in Jo'burg," says oom Thomas. "He played a bit of soccer here but he didn't have friends. He was always on his own."

"And Julius's dad? Where's he?"

Oom Thomas shakes his head. He doesn't know. Sello's dad never lived in the house next door. For a few seconds he looks at me without saying anything. "Do you know what the name means – 'Sello'?"

"No. What?"

"It means 'to cry'."

Back outside, the first thing I do, almost instinctively, is to check whether my bakkie is still on the pavement. The two youngsters are still sitting on the steps outside the Corner Store. They don't seem to be chatting. They aren't smoking or drinking either. They're just sitting.

Katrina Lebogo is the Malemas' neighbour on the other side. I knock on her door. She smiles when she hears the name "Sello" and walks across the worn linoleum in her sitting room to a table with a crocheted tablecloth. "Sello's place," she says and points to the head of the table. A Zion Christian Church badge glints on her chest.

Her Afrikaans and English are limited, but she tells me that her son Charles and Malema were boys together, that Malema sometimes came to eat here because they didn't have food next door.

After a while, Morris Dibetso, who has been hanging around outside, comes to interpret. Morris asks Katrina where Malema's father is and her reply contains many words. "Sello doesn't know his father," interprets Morris in a few words. "His mother was just playing with the man and then he gave her a child. Then that man was gone."

Katrina points to a tree in the garden of the Malemas' house and again utters many words while Morris interprets. "Sello didn't go around with friends. He used to sit under that tree by himself and talk of politics and sing songs, from when he was young."

At sixteen, Malema became the chairman of the Congress of South

African Students (Cosas) in Limpopo. He was over twenty when he passed matric.

As I walk back to the bakkie, I try to recall F.A. Venter's description of how a country can shape one's personality, but only bits and pieces come to me: ... *worms its way into your soul ... something subtle ... a father who can discipline you ... whom you will never leave ... live in a laager ...*

I look at the narrow streets and the small houses and wonder what it must have been like to grow up here like Malema did, without a father.

According to Katrina's directions, the Mohlakaneng High School that Malema attended from grade eight to grade twelve isn't far from here, past the Anglican church to a street that actually has a sign: Chris Hani Road.

Mohlakaneng High is clearly not a wealthy school. There's no sports field or pavilion in the school grounds.

Why is everyone making such a big deal of Malema's woodwork marks in matric? It's something that has stuck in the minds of so many of us: Malema, who got a GG for woodwork in matric. This, while he apparently got an H for maths.

Next to one of the buildings is a pile of broken tables and chairs. A small boy jogs past. Where's the woodwork classroom? He points to a classroom that stands to one side, away from the others.

The woodwork classroom always stands apart on the school grounds. It doesn't sound like a class is in progress. I peep in at the door. Inside, a man is marking question papers at a table. Is he the woodwork teacher?

The man nods and gets up. He introduces himself: Bopape – Mister M.E. Bopape.

Did he teach Julius woodwork? "Yes, of course," he replies. "He was in my class from grade eight to grade twelve."

There's a newspaper article on a pinboard. It's one that appeared last year when Malema was honoured by the school after he became president of the youth league.

Mister Bopape is hesitant to talk about Malema. It seems that Malema failed grade eight and had to repeat grade nine because he didn't allow his schoolwork to interfere with his political activities.

"Was Sello a good pupil, Mister Bopape?"

"He wasn't too bad."

"But didn't he get an H for woodwork?"

"You must remember, my friend. It's not me that gave him an H." It's other people who mark the end-of-year question papers. It's they who gave him an H.

Mister Bopape is getting slightly agitated. "Why do people talk so much? Why don't they leave Sello alone?"

He can't remember what mark *he* gave Malema in other exams. "But we don't have woodwork as a subject any more," he adds. "Woodwork is a thing of the past."

"Why, Mister Bopape? What happened to woodwork?"

"It's now called 'civil technology'."

On my way out of Masakeng I pass through Zone 1 again. I gather that Julius regularly comes to visit Ma Malema but seldom stays over

All that's really changed in Zone 1 in the past few years, it seems, is the house that he built. The flats. The streets are still riddled with potholes, the pavements are still unkempt and barren, and once a month oom Thomas and tannie Irene, the neighbours, go to stand in the pension queue and wait for mercy.

Katrina Lebogo, who helped babysit little Sello, has been without a job for a long, long time.

Wherever I go, I see people sitting and waiting – not just here in Polokwane. I begin my journey back to my pa, back into the interior, and everywhere people are waiting next to the road, in Mokopane and Bela-Bela and Brits and Rustenburg. They sit on plastic chairs outside mean little houses, they sit on steps and on cooldrink crates outside shops and spazas. They sit on rocks at big intersections and on the ground next to a broken-down bus by the roadside. They sit on pavements. They sit in funeral parlours, holding

146

dog-eared funeral books. They sit in cash loans places. They sit in clinics and hospitals and police stations and on upright benches in government buildings.

They are waiting.

34.

At the crossroads outside Masakeng I hesitate for a few moments: if I turned left, I'd be going further north, to Louis Trichardt, even deeper into the Bushveld. If I turn right, south. I'm hungry. I want to buy something to eat in Polokwane.

A little later, as I'm looking for a Spur or a Wimpy on the streets of Polokwane, my phone rings and I pull over into an empty parking bay. Johannes's name flashes on the screen. He mustn't start annoying me too, now.

"Yes, Johannes," I say. "What is it?"

It's not Johannes's voice on the other end. It's Pa's. "Hello, son."

"Why are you phoning from Johannes's phone, Pa?"

"I was afraid you were angry with me, son. I was afraid you wouldn't answer if you saw it was me."

Brakkenjan is barking in the background. Pa must be sitting at the kitchen table. I can see the crossword on the table, the radio with its coat-hanger aerial, the bowl with the oranges. On the wall, next to the fridge, hangs the church calendar.

"What are you doing?" I ask. "Are you all right?"

"I'm making macaroni cheese for us this evening."

Pa always uses the same oval glass dish to make macaroni cheese. He puts tomato slices on top and a lot of grated cheese that melts and always comes out of the oven slightly burnt.

And the table will be set with Ma's plates with the hairline cracks and the small red flowers.

"I'm going to set a place for you too, son," I hear Pa say after a while. "Come home. You belong here."

PART III

Nkandla

1.

Then Pa was gone. We buried him five days ago.

There were things I still wanted to tell him, but when I arrived in Ventersdorp rather worn out from the long trip and walked past the cement pond in the front garden, the smell of macaroni cheese wasn't in the air. The table wasn't set either. Pa was in his room on the bed, propped up against a stack of pillows, a bag of bones in Mr Price pyjamas. His breathing was shallow and rushed, like someone who is running up a hill. He could barely speak.

I was the bearer at the front right-hand side of the coffin and Johannes Bogotsi was at the back left. The Lord gave and the Lord took away, and now I'm sitting large as life in the study that Pa built for himself in the yard in Ventersdorp and have to decide the fate of a few hundred small books with red spines where he wrote every Sunday's sermon, and years worth of accumulated books and documents, brochures and leaflets, manuals, diplomas, certif-icates, souvenirs, LPs, tapes, a stuffed blue wildebeest head, a spring walk medal and a humongous crocheted Our Father in a plastic frame.

Among the books is F.A. Venter's *Werfjoernaal*. Another has also caught my eye: J.C. Steyn's *Die Verlore Vader*.

Like an index to Pa's life, everything is spread before me on the carpet, the desk, the shelves and on the walls. There's a faded election manifesto of the National Party, the New National Party, the Conservative Party, as well as a new one from the Democratic Alliance. There's the menu of the Rapportryer dinner that prime minister John Vorster signed on the evening in 1973 when he was guest speaker. There are slim booklets from the seventies that warn of the dangers of pop music and wearing patches that look like apples with a bite taken from them on the back of your jeans, against the Roman Catholic "Gevaar", the Black "Gevaar", the Yellow "Gevaar". There's a burgundy AWB beret, a whip that's been plaited by hand, an enlarged photograph of an ox-wagon at Blood River that was hewn from granite by the sculptor Coert Steynberg.

And all of this is a reflection of myself. This is how I grew up.

It is something subtle, invisible and intangible, a silent shaping of the heart and senses, like the spirit of a child in its parents' home.

I pick up the burgundy AWB beret and call: "Johannes!" He's unpacking a cupboard in the small room next to this one. He comes in. "Here's something for you." I hold out the beret.

He takes it and shoves it into the back of his trousers. He disappears back into the other room and returns with more stuff on the lid of a shoebox: a teaspoon, a pudding bowl, a funeral programme. "What must I do with this?" he asks.

The teaspoon's handle is decorated with the coat of arms of Aliwal North. Ma bought it that time we went to the hot springs in Aliwal. The pudding bowl Ouma bought for the inauguration of the Voortrekker Monument. On the funeral programme Oupa Danie, Pa's dad and the oupa I was named after, frowns from a faded photograph: Daniël Petrus Boshoff Snyman. *The Lord of Heaven and Earth has seen fit to take from us . . .*

Put it down here so long, I motion to Johannes. Before long, he's back with a small Zulu shield and a pitch-black doll with Zulu beads around her neck. "And this?" He laughs.

"Write it down," I hear oom Awie Smit from Vosburg, whom I'd seen two months ago, saying. "Write everything down."

"Bring my notebook from the room, Johannes."

The list gets very long. I write down even those things I throw away: a Weigh-Less booklet, a manual for a Hitachi tape recorder, a stack of *SA Panorama* magazines that were published by the government's department of information before 1994.

Johannes leaves the things that were on Pa's bedside table till last: a yellow Eveready torch, a bottle of Old Spice aftershave, the glass he used when he sometimes soaked his false teeth overnight, a pocket knife whose blade has been worn thin by all the sharpening. There's an article torn from a newspaper and a few loose sheets of paper with shopping lists and telephone numbers. One of them reads: *Museum in Pietermaritzburg*. With a phone number. I put the piece of paper in my pocket. Whether Pa phoned the museum to ask whether they really have great-grandpa Coenraad's trousers, I don't know.

I look at the newspaper article. Pa didn't simply rip it out. He used a ruler or a book to press down on the page and carefully and neatly tore it from the page.

Why did he keep this article? Did he maybe think I hadn't seen it, so he kept it for me?

I read it when it first appeared but now I read it again:

CAPE TOWN. – Afrikaners must find their own Nkandla.

Not a geographical area, but a psychological home where they are safe and have the freedom and confidence to live and express the things that are important to them.

President Jacob Zuma said yesterday in an interview with Beeld – the first with an Afrikaans newspaper since becoming president – that he has a deep understanding of the need of some Afrikaners for a home of their own.

"Take me as an example: I work in Cape Town and in Pretoria, but then I want to go to Nkandla (in rural KwaZulu-Natal). That's where I belong. I feel at home when I'm there. I can do the indlamu (a traditional dance for men), I can speak isiZulu. This is what some Afrikaners need on a psychological level: an Nkandla."

This article got Pa thinking, otherwise he wouldn't have torn it out. Did he lie on his bed or sit at the kitchen table and wonder where his Nkandla is – or was?

Or did he want to wait until we were sitting at the table, he and I, each with a plate of macaroni cheese and a glass of Grünberger Stein, to ask: "What do you think, son? Where is our Nkandla?"

Where the hell is it, Pa? I told you I don't always know best, Pa.

I fold the article in half and put it in my pocket with the piece of paper that has the museum's telephone number on it.

2.

Once again I see the day break somewhere on the open road. On the other side of Heidelberg, the horizon is brightening, like a light-bulb dimly shining behind a blue curtain. At Villiers I leave the N3 and head for Cornelia and Vrede and Memel.

At the house in Ventersdorp everything is more or less wrapped up, but there's one thing left for me to do before I head back to my own home in Jacobsbaai on the West Coast. Pa had wanted to visit Blood River, and Pietermaritzburg.

Why exactly he wanted to go there, I never discussed with him. Did he want to try and confirm who he was, one last time, and that the battle he and his people had fought here did have meaning?

Now I'm going there for Pa. Or rather, I'm going for both of us, for Pa and for me.

I'd travelled north from the Cape to try and discover why I sometimes feel like a stranger in my own country. It has something to do with a farewell to the old things, I know that now – a farewell to the old and an uncertainty about the new in the country. But it was a journey I had to make, I know, despite the sadness of leaving and the fear of the future.

I see Pa in the bakkie next to me, his walking stick between his knees and his grey Grasshoppers with the worn soles on his feet. Like the time two years ago, just before Christmas, when I took him to Memel so that he could retrace his steps with his walking stick and his Grasshoppers, resting every few paces.

Does our Nkandla lie even deeper into the interior, hey, Pa? Must we go looking for it?

Pa grew up in Memel. Oupa had a workshop there and Pa wrote matric there.

About five kilometres outside Vrede, on the way to Memel, I recognise the concrete picnic table where we'd sat that morning, two years ago, on our way there, and eaten the sandwiches and overboiled blueish eggs and sausages that he'd packed for us. The table is in an even greater state of disrepair, and rubbish is spilling from the round concrete rubbish bin.

Memel 40, it says on a road sign a little further along. Here the world is full of hills and mountains. In winter the frost kills the grass and the land is bleak, but now it's green and there are streams of water flowing between the hills. *Memel 30 . . .*

Perhaps Memel was Pa's Nkandla. Memel was Pa's putu pap and poor-boy flour-bag underpants and stories about going barefoot in the frost on a winter's morning – stories that had a happy ending when he stood with his cold feet in a heap of warm cow dung.

During Pa's last days, Johannes had to make him putu pap on the stove almost every morning.

Memel hasn't changed much since our visit. The Mayhem Guesthouse where we stayed is still here. So too is the building that housed Oupa's workshop, where the sign now reads: *Inguni Imphuphu*. Their old house in De Jager Street is still the colour of peanut butter, but I don't stop there. When Pa and I were here, the owner allowed us to walk through it. The wooden floor and pressed ceilings have long since become part of who I am.

In the main street I see the sign I photographed more than once on that trip:

Willems-Truter
Tar Avenue

There is something comical about it, because it's actually a very short stretch of tarred road – from the co-op to the Dutch Reformed church – that was given such a grand name. But on the other hand, if it weren't for this Willems and Truter, there may never have been a tar road here at all. All the other roads in town are untarred.

Throughout the country there are signs like this where people's names – usually men's – appear along roads, on bridges, outside church halls and town halls, in front of old-age homes and libraries and hospitals and clinics, at dams and factories.

Willems-Truter Tar Avenue, Bertie van Zyl Clinic, Boet van Drimmelen Bridge, Berdina Conradie Home for the Aged, Flippie Poggenpoel Dam.

Many of the people whose names appear on these signs belong to Pa's generation. All of them are old or dead now. They weren't without blame. They voted for laws that brought pain and suffering to others. Many of them helped to enforce those laws. But many of them, like Pa, were proud and hard-working too, because they believed you earn your bread by the sweat of your brow. Their handiwork can be seen throughout the country. They went to bed early and they rose early. They gave their tithes to the church and provided for children and lived from spring to summer to winter to autumn, and they believed that they would get their reward in the hereafter.

Against the wall of the high-school hall, near Memel's town centre, there's a large picture of the school badge: a hand plough with the sun rising behind it. The motto is: Watch and Work.

Pa was a child when the new school was built here, and each of the children was asked to design a badge for the school.

Pa's design, the one against that wall, is the design that won.

3.

About thirty kilometres before Dundee, a road sign points to the left: Blood River. Next to me, Pa raises his arm and points. I turn off onto a bumpy dirt road that rattles and rolls into the open veld, through a small drift, up an incline.

A little further along, another road sign announces it's nineteen kilometres to the battlefield. All along the road, the fences are anchored with corner posts cut from sandstone. Then I see a few buildings, and in the distance something that could be an ox-wagon laager.

Blood River.

To the south lies a mountain with a sandstone plateau. It's from here where the *amabutho*, the Zulu warriors who formed the left horn of the Zulu army's attack formation, approached on the morning of 16 December 1838. The Voortrekkers' wagons formed a laager on the western bank of the Ncome River. Inside the laager were four hundred and sixty-four men armed with muzzle loaders, under commander Andries Pretorius.

When the battle was over, only three of the men were wounded: Gerrit Raath, Philip Fourie and Pretorius, who'd been stabbed in the arm with an assegai. At least three thousand died in the battle.

It's as if all this information has suddenly popped up from somewhere deep in my memory. How many school projects haven't I done on the Battle of Blood River? How many exam questions have I answered? How many Day of the Covenant celebrations have I had to attend in my life?

Is there a name, a word, an event in the history of the Afrikaner that's more pregnant with meaning than Blood River?

The ox-wagon laager is quite a distance away from a rectangular flat-roofed building. In front of this building is the Coert Steynberg granite wagon, the one Pa had a photograph of on his study wall for who knows how long.

Then there's another sign pointing to another turn-off: Ncome Monument. Since 1998 there's been a second museum and place of remembrance at Blood River, one that was erected by President Nelson Mandela's government.

Which museum should you visit first? The old one? Or the new one?

The granite wagon is even bigger than it seemed in the photograph. The whole area, including the laager, is enclosed by that modern-day sign of a laager: a tall security fence. There's an electronic gate and an intercom at the entrance. To the side, an enormous notice board. *Visitors take note,* it announces in red letters. *The following rules apply when accessing and using the Blood River Site. 1. Only the official Covenant Commemoration . . .*

The gate slides open. The grass in front of the building has been cut and the geraniums and other plants in the beds and flowerpot are growing healthily. Inside the building, the smell of floor polish hangs in the air.

There's a restaurant and a shop where you can buy souvenirs. Towards the back is the museum section with a heavily varnished Voortrekker wagon, old Grietjie the cannon, a Dutch Bible, wash bowls and candleholders.

It feels as if I'm entering a part of me that I've been afraid to visit for a long time. Many of the homes from my youth had wash basins like these – a wash basin and a pitcher on the wash table with the marble top.

Pa's Dutch Bible, the one that belonged to Oupa, and before him my great-grandpa, will now be mine.

I look at the painting of Andries Pretorius hanging on the wall – the well-known one that shows him with his bandaged arm after the battle. For a long time I didn't think of the Voortrekkers as human beings; to me, they were the gods of my own Afrikaner realm: Pretorius, Piet Retief, Sarel Cilliers.

And great-great-great-grandpa Coenraad Frederik Wilhelmus Snyman, who was here at Blood River with Pretorius and Cilliers, was for me a sort of personal representative with Pretorius, Cilliers and the others. Fearless, god-fearing ooms, who had piercing looks and were crack shots with a muzzle loader.

I was aware of the Voortrekker women too, but they didn't have names. They were maternal, with quiet, sombre expressions. Just one had a name: Deborah Retief, Piet Retief's daughter.

Somewhere along the Voortrekkers' route, so we were taught, Deborah wrote her father's name on a rock near Harrismith. With green paint. I know the paint was green because every Zoom ice-cream sold just about anywhere in the seventies contained a card with a painting or sketch of a Voortrekker figure. On the card featuring Deborah, you could clearly see her writing her father's name in green.

The only other Voortrekker woman's name I'd ever heard was Grietjie – Grietjie, the cannon. Old Grietjie is here, in the museum. I stop and look at her.

How did the Voortrekkers go from being gods to ordinary people for me? It didn't happen overnight. It was a long road of asking questions and raising doubts about things I'd been taught since I was a boy.

Not that the Voortrekkers weren't a brave, remarkable group of people. Filled with faith and piety, they trekked into the interior, on a search for freedom, but here at Blood River they were also all too human, filled with revenge. The Voortrekkers took revenge on Dingaan's Zulus for the murder of Piet Retief and more than sixty of his men at Mgungundlovu ten months earlier on 6 February 1838. After that, the Zulus had also massacred another five hundred or so Voortrekker men, women and children at Bloukrans.

Shortly before the battle here at Blood River, Jan Bantjes, Pretorius's secretary, wrote in his journal: *To take revenge, because of the barbarous and inhumane murder of the former Leader of the Exiles, Pieter Retief, and his sixty companions, and the subsequent slaughter of men, women and children by Dingaan and his people . . .*

It's about a kilometre from the museum to the laager on the bank of the Ncome. The campsite is empty. I'm the only visitor here.

In my mind, a Day of the Covenant celebration is taking place.

In the platteland, these celebrations were often held in a special hall built in honour of the Day of the Covenant that was only used on 16 December each year. It wasn't really a hall; it was an enormous shed with a cement floor, and a kitchen at the back. You had to bring your own chair, and when you arrived you were given a roneoed copy of the programme where the proceedings were set out: Welcome. Scripture and prayer. Flag hoisting. Sermon. Oration.

Pa often took care of the scripture reading and prayer, in a black suit and a white shirt that was drenched with sweat and clung to his shoulders when everything was over.

No one ever made a speech at a Day of the Covenant celebration: there was an oration, often by a deputy minister with a carnation in his buttonhole. He read from small squares of paper and the oration contained phrases like: " . . . our godly responsibility here at the southern tip of Africa . . . tame the country . . . persevere in God's name . . . not bow one's neck under the same yoke with a heathen . . ."

I drive to the laager and stop when I get close. The silence, I notice the silence immediately – the same silence you often hear on a battlefield, a silence for which there's no explanation in the history books or in political speeches.

Was it the right thing to throw out the stack of *SA Panoramas* in Pa's study? It was in a *Panorama* that I first saw this laager – sixty-four wagons cast in copper. That was the era when a mother usually had her first-born's first pair of shoes cast in bronze. A whole ox-wagon made from copper – and sixty-four of them! – came close to being a miracle in my young eyes.

Outside the laager I linger a while. It's a clear, cloudless morning – much like the morning of 16 December 1838, after the mist of the night had cleared.

Sunday, the 16th of December, wrote Jan Bantjes in his diary. *The day is born before us; the sky is cloudless, the weather clear and bright.*

If you consider what the Day of the Covenant has come to mean through the years, it's ironic: probably the only reliable report of what happened here on that day is that of Jan Bantjes, and Jan was a coloured man who accompanied the Voortrekkers as a teacher and labourer. Jan Bantjes was a direct descendant of Hilletjie Agnita Jacobs van de Caab, a female slave.

Coenraad Frederik Wilhelmus Snyman, who was here with Jan, was a direct descendant of Groote Catrijn van de Caab, another female slave. Christoffel Snyman, the coloured forefather of the Snymans, was this oupa Coenraad's great-great-grandpa.

Oupa Coenraad's skin was the same shade of brown as Jan's.

What has happened? What caused the separation between white and coloured? The story is a long, complicated one of pride and shame and cruelty and stubbornness, and in a way I'm implicated. There was a time when I too voted for the National Party. I too lived and went to school in segregated suburbs, bought from segregated shops and swam at segregated beaches, and didn't rebel against it.

I enter the laager – and enter the silence. My great-great-great-grandpa must have stood somewhere around here on that morning, his eyes trained on the horizon. He was in danger, but how did his uncertainty about the future of the country differ from mine?

People died here.

For the most part, the battle was over by eleven that morning, writes Bantjes. Pretorius later ordered his men to try and count the Zulu bodies.

People prayed here and made promises to God. In this place, people experienced profound gratitude, profound exhaustion and a profound love for the land.

And now, after countless years and countless Day of the Covenant orations and flag-raising ceremonies, nothing remains except the silence.

The gate at the museum opens automatically. Then the noticeboard outside hits my eye again:

> Only the official Covenant Commemoration programme is allowed on the site annually over the period of 16 December. No other group or individual will be allowed to arrange any alternative commemoration programme on the site.
>
> The human dignity of all persons visiting the site must be respected at all times.
>
> Under no circumstances may other visitors to the site be interfered with.
>
> The right of admission will be reserved and persons who do not comply with the rules will be asked to leave the site immediately. Court orders that have been obtained to restrain certain individuals from entering the site will be enforced.
>
> The possession of firearms must be declared on arrival to Management.
>
> The carrying of exposed weapons is inadvisable. Weapons should be concealed at all times, in all areas on the site.
>
> Fauna and flora must be protected at all times.
>
> No stone cairn, commemoration, monument or structure may be erected on the site.
>
> The deliberate damage to any property on the site, or the disruption of an approved meeting, or the deliberate breach of any agreement with management or the commemoration organisers, will not be tolerated.

The Ncome site is about three kilometres by road from the laager. The road gradually becomes narrower and bumpier. This site is also fenced, but here a guard is sitting on a white plastic chair outside the gate. Next to him, a woman sits on the ground with a colourful blanket wrapped around her like a skirt.

The guard indicates that I can drive in at the gate.

Here, it seems, I'm once again the only visitor this morning. *Parking*, says a signpost. *Museum visitors only.*

I hear loud music coming from a grass hut next to the parking area, but the door is shut and it doesn't have windows. Next to the hut are three phone booths, a rather odd sight at a museum on a battlefield. Why three? Whom would one want to call from here?

There's no one here.

But someone must have been here earlier today, because inside the men's toilet – with a sign showing a Zulu warrior on the door – I see a sheet of paper with columns drawn on it stuck on the wall. Every morning, the person who comes to clean the toilets between 09:00 and 09:30 has to sign his name in one of the columns. One Sitondo signed it this morning, but now he's nowhere to be seen.

Near the entrance to the museum I see a mousetrap, one of those new types that uses a battery and shocks the mouse or something.

Inside, it's dusky and quiet. A Zulu warrior glares at me from inside a glass case. He's holding a shield.

"Bulalani abatakathi!" a warrior shouts somewhere in my mind. "Kill the white wizards!" That, we were taught from young, is what Dingaan shouted to his warriors just before they killed Retief and his men at Mgungundlovu.

In this museum the story of the battle of Blood River is told from the Zulus' perspective. There's also the story of the murder of Retief.

It is said that Retief and his company were loitering outside the king's palace on the evening of 5 February 1838, the clumsy Afrikaans on a card near the Zulu warrior reads. *It is not clear what they were doing. They may have wanted to attack the palace or to perform magic. Loitering outside someone's house after dark was seen as a serious offence in the Zulu kingdom, and interpreted as sorcery.*

Slowly, I walk past the display cases where Dingaan and his army are depicted. Then, at the exit, there's another case containing a small wooden box. Inside the box are an old pair of glasses, three keys on a small ring, and a few other bits and pieces. There's no connection with the Battle of Blood River. A typewritten card next to the box says: *This is a memory box, a project of the Siyazama Aids Trust.*

The Siyazama Aids Trust is a non-governmental organisation that works in the area. The people working for the trust help the children of mothers who are HIV positive or who have already died of Aids, to continue with their lives.

But why the glasses and keys?

There's another card next to the box. *It is accepted that it is right for a child to know his family history, however painful,* it says. *Knowing their parents' past enables children to cope better with their parents' death or illness. Each child is asked to write down the sick parent's story, and it is then kept in this box along with things that belonged to the parent.*

The things in this box are what reminded Nobuhle Ngema of her mother: a pair of glasses, a small ring with three keys, a packet of allergy pills, a bottle of cheap perfume, a beaded necklace.

I walk to the door. A yellow Eveready torch, a bottle of Old Spice aftershave, a pocketknife with a worn-down blade, a piece of paper on which is written: *Museum in Pietermaritzburg.*

And when I arrive outside, in the bright sunlight, I manage for the first time to cry about Pa's death.

4.

Gugu Dlamini behind the counter of the Vukaphanzi General Dealer in Nkandla can speak a little English. "This is Zuma's place." She finger points outside the door. "He born here."

On the shelf behind her are five tins of baked beans, a bag of sugar, six boxes of matches and a bottle of cooking oil. The cooldrink fridge is empty.

"His house. There. See."

The new buildings are set against the hill opposite the shop, three enormous kidney-shaped thatched houses, thirteen rondavels, and a small parking garage for around forty cars. "See. See."

President Jacob Zuma had this all built during the past few years, here in Nkandla, about fifty kilometres from Greytown, and had everything painted the same cream colour.

Here, where he was born and grew up, where one of his wives lives, where he married two of the others, where his parents are buried, and where twenty-four cattle were slaughtered on the day of his inauguration as president of South Africa.

Here, where he can speak Zulu and sit with the indunas of his clan and drink *ukombozi,* the traditional beer, and sometimes dance the *indlamu,* the traditional dance of Zulu men.

"He comes with helicopter." Gugu points to the sky.

Zuma's brother Joseph, according to Gugu, is the one who knows how things work in Nkandla. When the president isn't here, of course. Joseph lives on the other side of the hill, in his own house.

The hill is surrounded by a double security fence and there are rumbling machines and men in overalls everywhere, because the construction isn't finished: they're still busy with a presidential clinic and homes for the staff. It's believed the cost of the entire project is R65 million.

At the entrance to the president's place three policeman are chatting in the sun. Something that looks as if it could be a machine gun stands against the wall behind them. Visitors are very rarely allowed inside. Behind the hill, a road turns to the right.

The world around here is dotted with hills and ravines and basins and streams. The road runs next to the security fence, past more houses under construction, and goes up a hill. From the plateau they're easy to spot: two helipads. Five new tractors are parked around a scraggy little tree.

A bit further along, a man is standing next to a rather old Mazda bakkie outside four new rondavels, each of which has been fenced off. I pull over next to him. Maybe he'll know where I can find Joseph, the president's brother.

"Teddy Zuma," the man introduces himself. He points to a shabby little house and two rondavels lower down the hill – the hill next to the fenced-off presidential hill. That's Joseph's place.

All over the hillside there are small groups of round huts – rondavels – and small houses, often with a kraal made of branches.

President Zuma is Teddy's uncle. "My late father, Jobe, was the president's brother," he explains. "They are three brothers: my father, the president and Mike."

"And what about Joseph?" I point to the small house down the hill. "Isn't he the president's brother too?"

"He is. But with a different mother."

Teddy takes a twig, squats down, and tries to depict the Zuma clan by drawing lines in the earth. The president's father was Nobhekisisa Zuma, and he had two wives. The president's mother, Geinamazwi, was Nobhekisisa's second wife. Joseph is the son of Nobhekisisa's first wife.

Teddy tries to calculate how many children Nobhekisisa had with the two women, but before he can reach a total, he gets up and looks at his watch. "I'm late. We're actually on our way to a funeral."

A man comes out of one of the rondavels. He's holding a Zulu shield and a stick that he puts on the bakkie. Teddy points to another circle of rondavels. "I have to fetch my brother." He laughs. He can't say off the top of his head how many brothers and sisters he has. "There are too many because my dad cheated. He never married, but he got children from certain people. At the moment . . ." He starts to count his brothers and sisters on his fingers: there are six, with six different women.

Teddy has only one wife. "These days it's too expensive to have so many wives, but you have to understand, some men do things differently. It's part of Zulu culture. They call it *isithembu*. If you have only one wife, it means you're not a man."

Like other clan members, Teddy also sometimes goes to visit inside the security fence when the president is here. Sizakele Khumalo, the president's first wife, who he married in 1973, lives there more or less permanently. MaKhumalo, the people here call her. The president's other two wives, Nompumelelo Ntuli and Thobeka Mabhija, whom he married in two separate ceremonies here in Nkandla, come to visit regularly, as do some of his eighteen children.

Teddy walks over to his bakkie. It's eleven in the morning and the funeral started at ten o'clock. More people begin to appear and clamber in under the canopy.

It's only when I drive through the gate on my way out that I notice the sticker on the back of his bakkie of the WWE wrestler, The Undertaker.

Joseph Zuma's house is about five hundred metres from that of his brother, the president. With a double security fence between them.

Nothing in Joseph's yard is new: the wire fence is sagging, and weeds grow between the branches that form the kraal walls. Two empty cooldrink crates are stacked on top of each other. The walls of the house are crying out for a coat of paint, and five flip-flops and an empty Smirnoff vodka bottle are lying near the front door.

Manji, Joseph's daughter, appears in the door of the small house. Her English is shaky. She too speaks only Zulu, like almost everyone in these parts. Her dad isn't home, but she gives me his cellphone number. I call him while her mother, Tombi, the president's sister-in-law, fills the doorway behind her. She's wearing a T-shirt with the president's face on it as well as the words: "Zuma. My president."

I explain to Joseph that I've come here because the president said everyone in the country should have his own Nkandla. Now I want to learn more about his Nkandla.

"Just wait there," says Joseph on the phone. "Wait, wait, wait. I will come."

I go off and wait at the bakkie, and wait, and wait.

An hour or so later, Manji reappears from the house, this time holding a bottle of pink Brutal Fruit. She gives it to me and indicates that I should go with her.

"*Bulalani abatakathi!*" The voice is inside me. It just is.

Manji leads me though the front door. Inside, there's an old kitchen chair, a wooden bench, a fridge and a TV set. Nothing else. There's linoleum on the floor, just like there used to be in my ouma's kitchen.

And over everything hangs the smell of putu pap from a pot on the two-plate stove in the corner.

Manji motions for me to sit on the kitchen chair. Tombi is sitting on the linoleum with her legs stretched out in front of her, the president's face on her chest. Manji goes to sit next to her.

"*Sawubona.*" Although Pa could speak Zulu fluently, this is just about the only Zulu word I know.

"*Nikikona.*" They laugh. "*Unjane.*"

In a corner, a shield leans against the wall as well as an *isiquili* kierie which is used in traditional stick fights. Not far from it is a pair of shiny new men's shoes. Diagonally above it hangs a calendar of the Nazareth Baptist Church with a small photograph of the president on it. Through the window I can see a Toyota Prado on the presidential side of the fence.

169

A child – a little girl – comes crawling across the floor from one of the rooms. There are three fresh cuts on her face: one on the forehead and one on each cheek. The one on her forehead is still a little bloody.

It's her sister's child, Manji explains. She points to the cuts on the child's face. "It show she's Zuma. My mother she cut her."

Manji rubs her own cheek and forehead where faint scars are visible – scars that, it appears from the photograph, are on the president's face too, if you look closely.

Nobhekisisa, the president's father, died when he was four. The president never went to school in Nkandla, because there wasn't a school here. He tended the family's cattle, and together with his friends he hunted birds in the hills and killed snakes with his knobkierie.

The president's mother later went to work in Durban as a domestic worker, and from time to time he went to visit her. At seventeen he joined the ANC, and since then he has always come back to Nkandla to try to be again what he was brought up to be.

A bakkie arrives in the yard. Joseph. The president's brother. He enters the room quietly but doesn't take a seat. He's neither friendly nor unfriendly. "Who are you, my friend?" His eyes are piercing.

I explain: I write things down, I'm driving around the country, I come in peace.

"What Nkandla? This is Nkandla."

He hasn't read the newspaper article.

"You have your own Nkandla?"

Joseph checks his watch. "I must go to church."

He crosses his yard, passes the kraal here in his Nkandla, and walks to his bakkie as I walk to my bakkie and think of the Nkandlas where I'd grown up: the people in the houses may not always have had a lot of money, but their homes were clean and the garden gates were painted silver, proud little castles with a church calendar against the kitchen wall, where children learnt to work hard for what they wanted and to respect their elders and to be seen and not heard. All my Nkandlas always had a church, but in my Nka-

170

ndlas we also honoured and even worshipped our forefathers: Kruger, De la Rey, De Wet. In my Nkandlas we, too, were a tribe from Africa, a tribe among the other tribes in this country.

Joseph Zuma, one of the Zulus, gets into his bakkie, and I, an Afrikaner, get into my bakkie, and at the crossroads he turns left towards Eshowe; I turn towards Pietermaritzburg, and all of a sudden I feel lighter than I have in years. I drive past Greytown and past the turn-off to Weenen, and all the while I'm talking to Pa: our Nkandla is in our blood, Pa. It's almost like those long boring bits in the Bible: Christoffel is the son of Groote Catrijn and a German soldier, and he married a French girl, and she begat nine children, of which Philippus was the eldest; and Philippus married Johanna Margaretha van Deventer, and she bore a son and called him Jacobus. Thus the generations followed one after the other, through great-great-grandpa and grandpa, until it came to us. It's written in the archives, Pa. I saw it myself. And just think, Pa: the eldest of the first seven generations of Snymans, from Christoffel to Pa, had never been outside the country. Not once. Not even for a holiday. They were born here and their dust is now the country's dust.

I drive through plantations and past a lovely road that runs from Ixopo into the hills, and the hills are lovely beyond any singing of it, and down along the mountains in the direction of Pietermaritzburg: and a song erupts in me, a kind of Psalm for the optimistic traveller. My Nkandla is subtle, invisible and intangible. It's in the whisper of a bluegum, and in the maketh me to lie down in brown pastures of the Karoo. It's in the full moon on a church calendar. It's in the sound of a grandfather clock in the entrance hall and the three short and two long rings of a telephone in a farmhouse. It's in the aroma of a leg of lamb in the oven on a Sunday morning after church, and in the taste of a hard-boiled egg.

My Nkandla is it has pleased our Lord, our loving Father, to take on a funeral programme, and it's a toast to "tant Koek se hoenderhaan" at a wedding. It's in the calluses on the palm of a hand and in the worn sole of a Grasshopper shoe. It's in the blanket covering a mirror during a thunderstorm, and in the long unbroken peel of an orange peeled with a pocketknife.

My Nkandla is "gee, gee, gee, o, gee jou hart vir Afrikaans, gee jou sente, jou drome, jou toekoms vol gate". My Nkandla is wounded, it's in the fingerprint powder on the windows of a car or a house, it's in the white outlines around a lifeless body on the floor of a house. My Nkandla is burdened with the weight of guilt, of truncheons and guns and Casspirs, and hey, tata, go and live in a separate area, go and swim in another sea.

But my Nkandla is remorse and forgiveness too.

My Nkandla is in memories, but my Nkandla lies in the future too.

My Nkandla is in the great trek through the distances between people.

The Church of the Covenant is next to a taxi rank in the middle of Pietermaritzburg, opposite the Professor Nyembezi Centre. People and noise everywhere. At the gate a guard is sitting in a hut, because the grounds are in a fenced-off laager with points like spears.

The little church is behind a hall. A year after the battle of Blood River, in 1839, the Voortrekkers in Natal began collecting money to build this church. One of the first ministers to come here was reverend Daniel Lindley, the same Lindley that the town of Lindley in the Free State was named after. The church has a pitched roof, and on the square opposite there's a statue of Sarel Cilliers standing with his back to the taxi rank. With one hand he's pressing his hat to his chest; the other is shielding his eyes. He's looking north as if he's spotted danger approaching.

The door of the church is open, but in front of it is a security gate. A woman approaches from inside and then I'm inside too, among display cabinets and upright benches. But I don't see it anywhere. Could it just be a story Pa wanted to believe?

I see communion cups and whips and an anvil.

In a room at the back of the church I find it: great-great-great-grandpa's trousers – an enormous pair of trousers made from a coarse fabric. There they hang, large and wide, behind glass, as if he'd worn them just yesterday.

It feels as if he might walk in any minute and hug me with his large body and say: "Good grief, look who's here! Look who came to visit!"

Somewhere, the water for my coffee should be boiling in a blackened kettle on a coal stove. Somewhere, a feather mattress on a narrow iron bed should be waiting for me.

The room is as silent as the grave. I stand in front of the display cabinet with the trousers. Great-great-great-grandpa was clearly a big man. The Strongman of the Great Trek.

Below the trousers is a card that explains who great-great-great-grandpa was, in Afrikaans, English and Zulu.

Then I hear footsteps. A woman enters the room. She works here and when I tell her the trousers belonged to my great-great-great-grandfather she uses her cellphone to take a picture of me with the trousers. She reads the Zulu on the card out loud, and although I don't understand the words, I can tell that it's about a man from Africa, a member of a proud, determined race who made his mark here:

Ibhulukwe likaCoenraad Snyman owayenguMfunduki owaye-phethe enye yezinganono ezinkulu empini yaseNcome ngo 1838.

Then we begin talking, this woman and I; she talks and I talk to her, and I try to tell her about these trousers that are just a pair of trousers, but that are also more than a pair of trousers. I talk and talk and talk until she interrupts me. "From where are you?" she asks.

We go outside, the two of us, past the communion cups and the whip and the anvil. Once we're standing outside the church and the sharp-pointed laager, in the noisy taxi rank, surrounded by people, only then do I answer. "I am from here," I say. "This is where I come from."

Author's Note

For the most part, this book describes three trips I made through South Africa between January 2010 and June 2011. The characters are all real people I met along the way, and all the conversations really took place.

Most of the names I've used are real. In the few instances where I've changed a name, it's mainly because I lost one of my notebooks. My father in the book is my father, and Johannes Bogotsi is Johannes Bogotsi, who took care of my father towards the end of his life. The conversations between Pa and me are based on actual conversations we had.

To turn the stories into a single narrative, I had to change the time that elapsed between events. The bank robbery in Pofadder, for instance, took place much earlier than the farm murder at Lindley, something that is not clear from the book.

It may also be that I don't recall everything one hundred percent correctly. Is it really possible to see the ABSA bank from the Central Café in De Doorns? Suddenly, I'm no longer sure. There are a few other things I also doubt in hindsight. Nevertheless, I stand or fall by the "truth" of this book. This is the country as I experienced it. I travelled more than eight thousand kilometres in my bakkie to gather the information. I talked to many more people than is apparent from the story, and I probably damaged my health for good by eating countless suspect meat pies while on the road.

This book, like most, was written for selfish reasons. I wanted to explain the country and my place in it to myself. It was my journey, and when I speak, I speak for myself and no one else.

In the front of one of my notebooks – one I didn't lose – I copied a quotation from David Shields's book *Reality Hunger: A Manifesto*: "What is a fact? What's a lie, for that matter? What, exactly, constitutes an essay or a story or a poem or even an experience? What happens when we can no longer freeze the shifting phantasmagoria which is our actual experience?" This I had in the back of my mind the whole time. At some point a story takes on a life of its own, even a travel story like this one. But even if it was my own selfish trip, it happened with the support of people close to me. Every journey has its angels.

The publisher of this book, Erika Oosthuysen, was my guardian angel.

She encouraged me whenver I was ready to succumb to doubt. She helped by getting me an advance after I emailed her a picture of my broken-down bakkie from Strydenburg one morning. She never stopped believing in the book.

In a sense, Francois Smith, who read and edited the [original Afrikaans] text, and came up with suggestions, saw to it that my somewhat disjointed story became a book. It is difficult to express how big a part Francois played in this book. I will always be grateful to him.

My thanks go also to Max du Preez and Rian Malan for reading the manuscript.

A big thank you to Dr Erwin and Alta Coetzee of the Boekehuis in Calvinia who put me up for almost a month and allowed me to write undisturbed day in and day out, for free and without immediate worries. The Boekehuis is a very special place created by very special people. It was a privilege to stay there.

Also to Nardus Nel, for his friendship and encouragement. And thank you to Bun Booyens, for many reasons. And to Yvonne Beyers.

Ingrid, thank you for staying with me through this winter.

To everyone who talked to me along the way, and on farms and in towns, who tolerated me in their homes, thank you. Thank you to oom Japie Steenberg from Strydenburg, who let me stay in the asbestos igloo in his back yard for four days while he wrestled with my bakkie's wheel bearings in the winter cold.

It's impossible to travel eight thousand kilometres through this country and not return home filled with hope and a belief in the future.

This is where I'll stay, since I can't do otherwise.

Jacobsbaai, January 2012

PS: The quotations from F.A. Venter's *Werfjoernaal* are from the 1968 edition. The quotation from Etienne Leroux is taken from *Tussenspel,* published in 1980. In the last chapter I've used a short quotation from Alan Paton's *Cry, the Beloved Country,* taken from memory.

DANA SNYMAN was born in Stellenbosch. His father, oom Coenie, was a Dutch Reformed minister, one who accepted a call to yet another faraway small town every four years. As a result of this, Dana matriculated in the former Nylstroom.

After a brief, unsuccessful stint as university student, his CV lists, inter alia, jobs as a security guard, a switchboard operator and a book shop assistant. By the grace of God he landed a job in journalism, first as a crime reporter at *Beeld*, and then as a writer for *Huisgenoot*, where he covered everything from explosions to the *kettie* world championships. In 2004, he joined the travel magazine *Weg!* as travel writer, and worked there for four years.

Nowadays, Dana is a full-time author of books and articles for newspapers such as *Die Burger*, *Beeld* and *Volksblad*. He has also written three successful one-man shows for Frank Opperman. His stories have been published in four Afrikaans compilations – *Uit die binneland*, *Anderkant die scrap*, *Op die agterpaaie* and *Op die toneel*. *Op die agterpaaie* appeared in English as *On the Back Roads*.

When he's not on the road, Dana is at his home in Jacobsbaai with Jerry, Kleintjie and Vlooi, his beloved township-special dogs.

About Dana Snyman's work:

"The autobiography of a traveller who finds that the more he goes out to the country the more he travels inwards towards himself, who believes that one gets lost for a reason, this collection is also a warts-and-all biography of a people and a country . . . magical reportage." *The Sunday Times*

"Packed with authentic South African anecdotes . . . a gem." *YOU* magazine

"Searching for – and finding South Africa's secret soul." *Pretoria News*

"He captures the beauty of our diverse country and its people." *Essentials*

"Like his mentor, the writer Bruce Chatwin, he recognises an affinity between writing and travelling as forms of mental exploration . . . Intelligent and perceptive, he has an eye for illuminating social detail and a whimsical humour." *The Witness*

"All the stories speak of the enormous respect and sympathy Snyman has for his characters. The book changes one's outlook on everyday events and the people around you." Phyllis Green, *Sarie*

"This meandering, spontaneous watching and recording of that which lies behind the obvious reminds one of the posthumous work of Poland's most celebrated foreign correspondent, Ryszard Kapuściński." Rachelle Greeff, *Rapport*

"Dana Snyman is the representative of all of us. His compassionate look at ordinary people and their ways is not something that can be taught." Erns Grundlingh, *Insig*

"Dana Snyman is the chronicler, ironic, sardonic. His writing documents time for Everyman." Joan Hambidge, *Beeld*